PORTUGUESE

Phrase Book & Dictionary

HarperCollins*Publishers*

First published 1990
Copyright © HarperCollins Publisher
Reprint 10 9 8 7 6 5 4 3 2
Printed in Italy by Amadeus SpA, Rome
ISBN 0 00-435871-6

INTRODUCTION

Your *Collins Phrase Book and Dictionary* is a handy, quick-reference guide that will help you make the most of your stay abroad. Its clear layout, with direct alphabetical access to the relevant information, will save you valuable time when you need that crucial word or phrase.

There are two main sections in this book:

- 70 practical topics arranged in A-Z order from **ACCIDENTS** to **WINTER SPORTS** via such subjects as **MENUS, ROOM SERVICE** and **TAXIS**. Each topic gives you the basic phrases you will need along with clear but simple pronunciation guidelines. In many cases, there's the added bonus of our 'Streetwise' travel tips – practical and often invaluable travel information.

  And, if you've found the right phrase but still need a vital word, you're sure to find it in the final topic, **WORDS**, a brief but rigorously practical list of English words and their translations, chosen for their relevance to the needs of the general traveller.

- A 4000-word foreign vocabulary; the key to all those mystifying but important notices, traffic signs, menus, etc which confront the traveller at every turn. This mini-dictionary will help you enjoy to the full the country's cuisine, save you time with asking directions, and perhaps prevent you getting into one or two tricky situations!

So, just flick through the pages to find the information you require. Why not start with a quick look at the **GRAMMAR, ALPHABET** and **PRONUNCIATION** topics? From there on the going is easy with your *Collins Phrase Book and Dictionary*.

Bom viagem!

LIST OF TOPICS

Streetwise

In the event of a serious accident you should call the police (115). Otherwise, ask for the other person's insurance policy and make a note of the number, together with the car's registration. Remember also that it is compulsory for you to carry a red warning triangle in case of breakdowns or accidents.

There's been an accident	**Houve um acidente** *ohv oom asee**dent***
I've crashed my car	**Tive um choque com o meu carro** *teev oom shok kong oo **mayoo karroo***
Can I see your insurance certificate?	**Posso ver o seu seguro?** ***poss**oo vehr oo **say**-oo suh**goo**roo*
We will have to report it to the police	**Temos que comunicar à polícia** ***tay**-moosh kuh koomoonee-**kar** a poo**leess**-yuh*
He ran into me	**Ele chocou contra mim** *ayl shoo**koh kon**truh meeng*
He was driving too fast	**Ele vinha em alta velocidade** *ayl **veen**-yuh ayng **al**tuh veloo-see**dahd***
He was too close	**Ele estava demasiado perto de mim** *ayl **shtah**-vuh duh-muh-zee-**ah**-doo **pehr**too duh meeng*
He did not give way	**Ele não deu prioridade** *ayl nowng **day**-oo pree-oree-**dahd***
The car number was ...	**A matrícula do carro era ...** *uh ma-**tree**kooluh doo **karr**oo **eh**ruh ...*

See also **BREAKDOWNS, EMERGENCIES**

ACCIDENTS – INJURIES

Streetwise

There has been an accident	**Houve um acidente** *ohv oom aseedent*
Call an ambulance/ a doctor	**Chame uma ambulância/um médico** *shahm oomuh amboolanss-yuh/oom medikoo*
He has hurt himself	**Ele feriu-se** *ayl fer-yoo-suh*
I am hurt	**Estou ferido** *shtoh fereedoo*
He can't breathe/ move	**Ele não pode respirar/mexer-se** *ayl nowng pod rushpeerar/mushehr-suh*
I can't move my arm/leg	**Não posso mexer o braço/a perna** *Nowng possoo mushehr oo brah-soo/uh pehr-nuh*
Cover him up	**Cubram-no** *koobrowng-noo*
Don't move him	**Não lhe mexam** *nowng l-yuh meshowng*
He has broken his arm/cut himself	**Ele partiu o braço/cortou-se** *ayl part-yoo oo brah-soo/koortoh-suh*
I have had a fall	**Dei uma queda** *day oomuh keduh*

See also **EMERGENCIES**

Streetwise

I want to reserve a single/double room	**Quero reservar um quarto individual/um quarto de casal** *kehroo ruh-zervar oom kwartoo eendeeveed-wal/oom kwartoo duh kazal*
Do you have facilities for the disabled?	**Tem instalçoes para deficientes?** *tayng een-shtalluh-soynsh paruh duh-feess-yentsh*
I want bed and breakfast/full board	**Quero dormida e pequeno almoço/ pensão completa** *kehroo door-meeduh ee puh-kaynoo almoh-soo/ pensowng kompletuh*
What is the daily/ weekly rate?	**Qual é a diária?/Quanto custa por semana?** *kwal e uh dee-ar-yuh/kwantoo kooshtuh poor semah-nuh*
I want to stay three nights/from … till …	**Quero ficar três noites/do dia … ao dia …** *kehroo feekar traysh noytsh/doo dee-uh … ow dee-uh …*
We'll be arriving at …/very late	**Vamos chegar ás …** (*see* TIME)**/muito tarde** *vah-moosh shuh-gar ash …/mweentoo tard*

See also **CAMPING, HOTEL DESK, ROOM SERVICE, SELF-CATERING**

Where do I check in for the flight to London?

Onde faço a check-in para o voo de Londres?
onduh fah-soo oo check-in paruh oo voh-oo duh londrush

I'd like an aisle/a window seat

Gostava de um lugar perto da coxia/da janela
gooshtah-vuh doom loogar pehrtoo duh kooshee-uh/duh janeluh

Will a meal be served on the plane?

Vão servir uma refeição no avião?
vowng serveer oomuh ruh-fay-sowng noo av-yowng

Where is the snack bar/duty-free shop?

Onde fica o snack-bar/a free-shop?
onduh feekuh oo snack-bar/uh free-shop

Where can I change some money?

Onde posso cambiar dinheiro?
onduh possoo kamb-yar deen-yay-roo

Where do I get the bus to town?

Onde se apanha o autocarro para a cidade?
onduh see apahn-yuh oo owntoo-karroo pra seedahd

Where are the taxis/telephones?

Onde ficam os táxis/os telefones?
onduh feekwong oosh taxeesh/oosh tuh-luh-fonsh

I want to hire a car/reserve a hotel room

Quero alugar um carro/reservar um quarto
kehroo aloogar oom karroo/ruh-zervar oom kwartoo

I am being met

Estão à minha espera
shtowng a meen-yuh shpehruh

The Portuguese alphabet is the same as the English one, with the exception of three letters: K, W and Y. These letters are only used in foreign words that have come into use in Portuguese.

A *a*	como *koh-moo*	**Alexandre** *aluh-shandruh*	**N** *en*	come *koh-moo*	**Nicolau** *neekooo-la-oo*
B *bay*		**Banana** *banah-nuh*	**O** *oh*		**Óscar** *oshkar*
C *say*		**Carlos** *karloosh*	**P** *pay*		**Paris** *pareesh*
D *day*		**Daniel** *dan-yel*	**Q** *kay*		**Quarto** *kwartoo*
E *ay*		**Eduardo** *eedwardoo*	**R** *err*		**Ricardo** *reekardoo*
F *ef*		**França** *fransuh*	**S** *ess*		**Susana** *soozanuh*
G *jay*		**Gabriel** *gabree-el*	**T** *tay*		**Teresa** *tuh-ray-zuh*
H *aga*		**Holanda** *oh-landuh*	**U** *oo*		**Ulisses** *ooleesush*
I *ee*		**Itália** *eetal-yuh*	**V** *vay*		**Venezuela** *vuh-nuh-zway-luh*
J *jotuh*		**José** *jooze*	**X** *sheesh*		**Xangai** *shang-gye*
L *el*		**Lisboa** *leejboh-uh*	**Z** *zay*		**Zebra** *zebruh*
M *em*		**Maria** *maree-uh*			

ASKING QUESTIONS

Is it far/expensive?	**Fica longe?/É caro?** *feekuh lonj/e kah-roo*
Do you understand?	**Compreende?** *kompree-end*
Can I go in there?	**Posso lá entrar?** *possoo la ayn-trar*
Can you help me?	**Pode ajudar-me?** *pod ajoodar-muh*
Where is the chemist's?	**Onde fica a farmácia?** *onduh feekuh uh farmass-yuh*
Where are the toilets?	**Onde é a casa de banho?** *ondee e uh kah-zuh duh bahn-yoo*
How do I get there?	**Como se vai para lá?** *koh-moo suh vy paruh la*
How far/big is it?	**A que distancia fica?/Que tamanho tem?** *uh kuh deesh-tanss-yuh feekuh/kuh taman-yoo tayng*
Is there a good restaurant?	**Há um bom restaurante?** *a oom bong rushtoh-rant*
What is this?	**O que é isto?** *oo kee e eeshtoo*
How much is it?	**Quanto custa?** *kwantoo kooshtuh*
How many kilometres?	**Quantos kilómetros?** *kwantoosh kee-lometroosh*

Streetwise

A red flag on a Portuguese beach means that it is dangerous to go swimming. A yellow flag means that you can swim, but it is not recommended. If you see a green flag, go right ahead!

Is it safe to swim here?	**Não há perigo de nadar aqui?** *nowng a pereegoo duh nadar akee*
When is high/low tide?	**Quando é a maré-alta/a maré-baixa?** *kwandoo e uh mare-altuh/uh mare-by-shuh*
Is the water deep?	**É fundo?** *e foondoo*
Are there strong currents?	**Há correntes fortes?** *a koo-rentsh fortsh*
Is it a private/quiet beach?	**É uma praia particular/sossegada?** *e oomuh pry-uh parteekoo-lar/soo-suh-gah-duh*
Where do we change?	**Onde é que nos mudamos?** *ondee e kuh noosh moodah-moosh*
Can I hire a deck chair/a boat?	**Posso alugar uma cadeira de lona/um barco?** *possoo aloogar oomuh kaday-ruh duh lonuh/oom barkoo*
Can I go fishing/windsurfing?	**Posso ir pescar/fazer windsurf?** *possoo eer pushkar/fazehr windsurf*
Is there a children's pool?	**Há uma piscina para crianças?** *a oomuh peesh-seenuh paruh kree-ansush*
Where can I get an ice cream?	**Onde é que há gelados?** *ondee e kee a jelah-doosh*

BREAKDOWNS

Streetwise

In the case of a breakdown you should phone for assistance from the nearest SOS phone point. On motorways and main roads these are placed at three-kilometre intervals. On other roads use a normal phone to call (dial 115) for the police, ambulance or the fire brigade. The ACP (Automovel Clube de Portugal) has reciprocal agreements with British and other foreign motoring organisations. Don't forget you must carry a red warning triangle at all times and place it 50 m behind your car when you have a breakdown.

My car has broken down	**O meu carro avariou-se** *oo **may**oo **karr**oo avaree-**oh**-suh*
There is something wrong with the brakes	**Os travões não funcionam bem** *oosh tra**voynsh** nowng foonsee-**on**owng bayng*
I have run out of petrol	**Acabou-se-me a gasolina** *akuh-**boh**-suh-muh uh gazoo-**lee**nuh*
There is a leak in the radiator/petrol tank	**Há uma ruptura no radiador/depósito da gasolina** *a **oom**uh roop**too**ruh noo radee-uh-**dor**/ duh-**poz**itoo duh gazoo-**lee**nuh*
The engine is overheating	**O motor aquece demais** *oo moo**tor** a**kess** duh-**mysh***
Can you tow me to a garage?	**Pode rebocar-me para uma garagem?** *pod ruh-boo**kar**-muh **proom**uh ga**rah**-jayng*
Can you send a mechanic/a breakdown van?	**Pode mandar um mecânico/um pronto socorro?** *pod man**dar** oom muh-**kahn**ikoo/oom prontoo soo**korr**oo*
Do you have the parts?	**Tem as peças?** *tayng ush **pess**ush*

Streetwise

I have an appointment with …	**Tenho um encontro com …** *ten-yoo oom ayng-**kon**troo kong …*
He is expecting me	**Ele está à minha espera** *ayl shta a **mee**nyuh **shpeh**ruh*
Can I leave a message with his secretary?	**Posso deixar um recado à secretária?** ***poss**oo day-**shar** oom re**kah**-doo a sekruh-**tar**-yuh*
I am free tomorrow morning/for lunch	**Estou livre amanhã de manhã/para almoçar** *shtoh **lee**vruh aman**yang** duh man**yang**/**pa**ruh almoo**sar***
Can I send a telex from here?	**Posso mandar um telex daqui?** ***poss**oo man**dar** oom telex da**kee***
Where can I get some photocopying done?	**Onde é que eu posso fazer fotocópias?** *ondee e kee **ay**-oo **poss**oo fa**zehr** footoo-**kop**-yush*
I want to send this by courier	**Quero mandar isto por um mensageiro** ***keh**roo man**dar** **eesh**too poor oom mensa-**jay**-roo*
I will send you further details/a sample	**Vou-lhe mandar mais pormenores/uma amostra** *voh-l-yuh man**dar** mysh poormuh-**nor**ush/**oom**uh a**mosh**-truh*

BUYING

Streetwise

Do you sell stamps?
Vende selos?
*vend **say**-loosh*

How much is that?
Quanto custa?
***kwan**too **koosh**tuh*

Have you anything bigger/smaller?
Tem maior/mais pequeno?
*tayng ma-**yor**/mysh puh-**kay**-noo*

Have you got any bread/matches?
Tem pão/fósforos?
tayng powng fosh-tooroosh

I'd like a newspaper/some apples
Quero um jornal/maças
kehr**oo oom joornal/ma**sansh

A packet of cigarettes, please
Um maço de cigarros, por favor
*oom **mah**-soo duh see-**gar**roosh poor fa**vor***

I prefer this one
Prefiro este
*pruh-**fee**roo aysht*

I'd like to see the one in the window
Quero ver aquele que está na montra
***kehr**oo vehr a**kayl** kuh shta nuh **mon**truh*

I'll take this one/that one there
Levo este/aquele
lev**oo aysht/a**kayl

Could you wrap it up for me, please?
Pode embrulhar, por favor?
*pod aymbrool-**yar** poor fa**vor***

See also **PAYING, SHOPPING**

Streetwise

Portugal has many official camp sites and all provide a full range of facilities. You are advised to use these and not camp anywhere else without permission.

We are looking for a camp site
Procuramos um parque de campismo
*prookoo-**rah**-mooz oom park duh kam-**peej**-moo*

Do you have any vacancies?
Tem lugares vagos?
*tayn loo**gah**-rush **vah**-goosh*

How much is it per night?
Quanto custa por noite?
***kwan**too **koosh**tuh poor noyt*

We want to stay one night
Queremos ficar uma noite
***kray**-moosh fee**kar oom**uh noyt*

May we camp here?
Podemos acampar aqui?
*poo**day**-moosh akam**par** a**kee***

Can we park our caravan there?
Podemos estacionar a caravana ali?
*poo**day**-moosh shtass-yoo**nar** uh kara**vah**-nuh a**lee***

Is there a shop/a restaurant?
Há alguma loja/algum restaurante?
*a al**goo**muh **loj**uh/al**goom** rushtoh-**rant***

Where is the washroom?
Onde fica a casa de banho?
***on**duh **fee**kuh uh **kah**-zuh duh **bahn**-yoo*

What facilities do you have on the site?
Que instalações tem o parque de campismo?
*kuh een-shtaluh-**soynsh** tayng oo park duh kam-**peej**-moo*

CAR HIRE

Streetwise

I want to hire a car	**Quero alugar um carro** *kehroo aloogar oom karroo*
I need a car with a chauffeur	**Preciso de um carro com condutor** *pre-seezoo doom karroo kong kondootor*
I want a large/small car	**Quero um carro grande/pequeno** *kehroo oom karroo grand/puh-kaynoo*
Is there a charge per kilometre?	**Há alguma taxa por quilómetro?** *a algoomuh tashuh poor kee-lometroo*
How much extra is the comprehensive insurance cover?	**Quanto é que tenho que pagar mais para ter um seguro contra todos os riscos?** *kwantoo e kuh ten-yoo kuh pagar mysh paruh tehr oom segooroo kontruh toh-duz oosh reeshkoosh*
I would like to leave the car in Lisbon	**Gostava de deixar o carro em Lisboa** *gooshtah-vuh duh day-shar oo karroo ayng leej-boh-uh*
My husband/My wife will be driving as well	**O meu marido/a minha mulher também vai conduzir** *oo mayoo mareedoo/uh meen-yuh mool-yehr tambayng vy kondoo-zeer*
How do I operate the controls?	**Como funcionam os comandos do carro?** *koh-moo foonss-yonowng oosh koo-mandoosh doo karroo*

Streetwise

Remember that no photographic materials are sold at chemists' (farmácias) in Portugal, and only certain kinds of toiletries like face creams or babies' toiletry items are available. For the more usual toiletries you should look for a perfumaria or a drogaria. Opening times are as for other shops. For details of chemists' open outside normal hours, look for the sign 'escala de turnos para serviço permanente' on display at all chemists'.

I want something for a headache/a sore throat/toothache	**Quero qualquer coisa para as dores de cabeça/de garganta/de dentes** *kehroo kwal-**kehr koy**zuh prash **dor**ush duh ka**bays**uh/duh gar**gan**tuh/duh dentsh*
I would like some aspirin/sticking plaster	**Quero aspirinas/pensos** *kehroo ashpee-**ree**nush/**pen**soosh*
Have you anything for insect bites/sunburn/diarrhoea?	**Tem alguma coisa para as mordeduras de insectos/as queimaduras/a diarreia?** *tayng al**goo**muh **koy**zuh prash morduh-**doo**rush deen-**sek**toosh/ush kaymuh-**doo**rush/ uh dee-uh-**ray**uh*
I have a cold/a cough	**Estou constipado/Tenho tosse** *shtoh kon-shteepah-doo/**ten**-yoo tohss*
How much/how many do I take?	**Quanto/quantos tomo?** ***kwan**too/**kwan**toosh **tom**oo*
How often do I take it?	**Quantas vezes o tomo?** ***kwan**tush **vay**-zuz oo **tom**oo*
Is it safe for children?	**Não há perigo para as crianças?** *nowng a pe**ree**goo prash kree-**an**sush*
How do I get reimbursed?	**Como é que posso ser reembolsado?** ***koh**-moo e kuh **poss**oo sehr ree-aymbol-**sah**-doo*

CHILDREN

Streetwise

I have two children

Tenho duas crianças
*ten-yoo **doo**-ush kree-**an**sush*

Do you have a special rate for children?

Há um preço especial para crianças?
*a oom **pray**-soo shpuss-**yal pa**ruh kree-**an**sush*

Do you have facilities for children?

Tem instalações para crianças?
*tayng een-shtaluh-**soynsh pa**ruh kree-**an**sush*

Have you got a cot for the baby?

Tem um berço para o bebé?
*tayng oom **behr**-soo pro bebe*

Do you have a special menu for children?

Tem uma ementa especial para crianças?
*tayng **oom**uh ee**men**tuh shpuss-**yal par**uh kree-**an**sush*

Where can I feed/ change the baby?

Onde é que posso dar de comer ao bebé/mudar o bebé?
*on*dee e kuh **poss**oo dar duh koo**mehr** ow bebe/moo**dar** oo bebe*

Where can I warm the baby's bottle?

Onde é que posso aquecer o biberão do bebé?
*on*dee e kuh **poss**oo ake**sehr** oo beebuh-**rowng** doo bebe*

Streetwise

Catholicism is the principal religion in Portugal. You will find the times of church services in the local press. Other religions are also practised and in many areas you should be able to find other kinds of churches. When attending church, or even just visiting as a tourist, dress should be fairly formal – short skirts and even short-sleeved shirts are considered disrespectful.

Where is the nearest church?	**Onde fica a igreja mais próxima?** *onduh feekuh uh ee-grejuh mysh prosseemuh*
Where is there a Protestant church?	**Onde é que há uma igreja protestante?** *onduh e kee a oomuh ee-grejuh prootush-tant*
I want to see a priest	**Quero falar com um padre** *kehroo falar kong oom padruh*
What time is the service?	**A que horas é a missa?** *uh kee oruz e uh meessuh*
I want to go to confession	**Quero-me confessar** *kehroo-muh komfesar*

CITY TRAVEL

Streetwise

Buy your tickets at the entrance to the bus or the underground. On a bus you must then clip your ticket in the machine provided. Buses in cities usually have a flat fare. If you are making a number of journeys, you can buy a book of tickets (caderneta) from newspaper kiosks or underground stations. You can also get a day travelcard in large cities.

Does this bus/train go to …?	**Este autocarro/comboio vai para …?** *aysht owtoo-**karr**oo/kom-**boy**oo vy **par**uh …*
Which number bus goes to …?	**Qual é o número do autocarro que vai para …?** *kwal e oo **noo**meroo doo owtoo-**karr**oo kuh vy **par**uh …*
Where do I get a bus for the airport?	**Onde é que posso apanhar o autocarro para o aeroporto?** ***on**dee e kuh **poss**oo apan-**yar** oo owtoo-**karr**oo pro uh-ehroo-**por**too*
Where do I change/ get off?	**Onde é que mudo/desço?** ***on**dee e kuh **moo**doo/**desh**-soo*
Where is the nearest underground station?	**Onde fica a estação de metro mais próxima?** ***on**duh feek ushta-**sowng** duh **me**troo mysh **pross**imuh*
What is the fare to the town centre?	**Quanto custa o bilhete para o centro da cidade?** ***kwan**too **koosh**tuh oo beel-**yet** pro **sen**troo duh see**dahd***
Where do I buy a ticket?	**Onde é que compro um bilhete?** ***on**dee e kuh **kom**proo oom beel-**yet***

Is there a laundry service?

Há um serviço de lavandaria?
*a oom ser-**vee**soo duh lavanduh-**ree**-uh*

Is there a launderette/ dry-cleaner's nearby?

Há uma lavanderia/limpeza a seco aqui perto?
*a **oom**uh lavanduh-**ree**-uh/leem**pay**-zuh uh **say**-koo a**kee** pehrtoo*

Where can I get this skirt cleaned/ironed?

Onde é que posso mandar limpar/passar a ferro esta saia?
*on**dee** e kuh **poss**oo man**dar** leem**par**/pa**sar** uh **ferr**oo **esht**uh sy-uh*

I need to wash this off immediately

Preciso de tirar isto urgentemente
*pre-**see**zoo duh tee**rar** **eesht**oo oorjent-**ment***

Where can I do some washing?

Onde é que posso lavar a roupa?
*on**dee** e kuh **poss**oo la**var** uh **roh**-puh*

I need some soap and water

Preciso de sabão e água
*pre-**see**zoo duh sa**bowng** ee **ahg**-wuh*

Where can I dry my clothes?

Onde é que posso secar a roupa?
*on**dee** e kuh **poss**oo se**kar** uh **roh**-puh*

This stain is coffee/ blood

Esta nódoa é de café/sangue
***esht**uh **nod**-wuh e duh kuh-**fe**/**sang**uh*

Can you remove this stain?

Pode tirar esta nódoa?
*pod tee**rar** **esht**uh **nod**-wuh*

It is very delicate

É muito delicado
*e **mween**too duh-lee-**kah**-doo*

When will my things be ready?

Quando é que está pronto?
***kwan**doo e kuh shta pront*

CLOTHES

I take a size 40	**O meu número é o quarenta** *oo **may**oo **noom**eroo e oo kwa**ren**tuh*
Can you measure me, please?	**Pode medir-me, por favor?** *pod me**deer**-muh poor fa**vor***
May I try on this dress?	**Posso experimentar este vestido?** ***poss**oo shpuh-reemen**tar** aysht vush**teed**oo*
May I take it over to the light?	**Posso vê-lo à luz?** ***poss**oo veh-loo a loosh*
Where are the changing rooms?	**Onde ficam os gabinetes de provas?** ***on**duh **fee**kowng oosh gabee-**netsh** duh **prov**ush*
Is there a mirror?	**Há um espelho?** *a oom **shpel**-yoo*
It's too big/small	**Fica-me muito grande/pequeno** ***fee**kuh-muh **mween**too grand/puh-**kay**-noo*
What is the material?	**Qual é a fazenda?** *kwal e uh fa**zen**duh*
Is it washable?	**É lavável?** *e la**vah**-vel*
I don't like it/them	**Não gosto** *nowng **gosh**too*
I don't like the colour	**Não gosto da cor** *nowng **gosh**too duh kor*

Streetwise

The state-run coach company, Rodoviária Nacional, provides a highly efficient service and private companies also operate in most large cities. In all, the coach services constitute a network much larger than that of the railway system. Travelling by coach is also cheaper than going by train and more versatile as regards routes and services. Videos are shown on longer journeys.

Is there a bus to …?	**Há algum autocarro para …?** *a algoom owtoo-karroo paruh …*
Which bus goes to …?	**Qual é o autocarro que vai para …?** *kwal e oo owtoo-karroo kuh vy paruh …*
Where do I catch the bus for …?	**Onde é que posso apanhar o autocarro para …?** *ondee e kuh possoo apan-yar oo owtoo-karroo paruh …*
What are the times of the buses to …?	**A que horas partem os autocarros para …?** *uh kee orush partayng ooz owtoo-karroosh paruh …*
Does this bus go to …?	**Este autocarro vai para …?** *aysht owtoo-karroo vy paruh …*
Where do I get off?	**Onde é que desço?** *ondee e kuh desh-soo*
Is there a toilet on board?	**O autocarro tem casa de banho?** *oo owto-karroo tayng kah-zuh duh bahn-yoo*
Is there an overnight service to …?	**Há um autocarro à noite para …?** *a oom owtoo-karroo a noyt paruh …*
What time does it leave/arrive?	**A que horas é que parte/chega?** *uh kee oruz e kuh part/shay-guh*

COMPLAINTS

This does not work	**Isto não funciona** *eeshtoo nowng foonss-yonuh*
I can't turn the heating off/on	**Não consigo desligar/ligar o aquecimento** *nowng konseegoo duj-leegar/leegar oo akussee-mentoo*
The lock is broken	**A fechadura está partida** *uh feshuh-dooruh shta par-teeduh*
I can't open the window	**Não posso abrir a janela** *nowng possoo abreer uh janeluh*
The toilet won't flush	**O autoclismo não trabalha** *oo owtoo-kleej-moo nowng trabal-yuh*
There is no hot water/toilet paper	**Não há água quente/papel higiénico** *nowng a ahg-wuh kent/papel eej-yenikoo*
The washbasin is dirty	**O lavatório está sujo** *oo lavuh-tor-yoo shta soojoo*
The room is noisy	**O quarto é barulhento** *oo kwartoo e barool-yentoo*
My coffee is cold	**O meu café está frio** *oo mayoo kuh-fe shta free-oo*
We are still waiting to be served	**Ainda estamos à espera que nos sirvam** *a-eenduh shtah-mooz a shpehruh kuh noosh seervowng*
I bought this here yesterday	**Comprei isto aqui ontem** *kompray eeshtoo akee ontayng*
It has a flaw/hole in it	**Tem um defeito/um buraco** *tayng oom duh-fay-too/oom boorah-koo*

Streetwise

People usually shake hands when they meet and also when they say goodbye. Between close female acquaintances and relatives a kiss on both cheeks is the customary greeting.

How do you do?	**Como está?** *koh-moo shta*
Hello	**Olá** *oh-la*
Goodbye	**Adeus** *aday-oosh*
Do you speak English?	**Fala inglês?** *fah-luh eenglesh*
I don't speak Portuguese	**Não falo português** *nowng fah-loo poortoo-gesh*
What's your name?	**Como se chama?** *koh-moo suh shah-muh*
My name is …	**Chamo-me …** *shah-moo-muh …*
Do you mind if I sit here?	**Importa-se se eu me sentar aqui?** *eemportuh-suh see ay-oo muh sentar akee*
I'm English/Scottish/Welsh/Irish	**Sou inglês/escocês/galês/irlandês** *soh eenglesh/shkoosesh/galesh/eerlan-desh*
Are you Portuguese?	**É português?** *e poortoo-gesh*
Would you like to come out with me?	**Quer sair comigo?** *kehr suh-eer koomeegoo*

CONVERSATION 2

| Yes please | **Sim, por favor** |
| | *seeng poor fa**vor*** |

| No thank you | **Não, obrigado** |
| | *nowng oh-bree**gah**-doo* |

| Thank you (very much) | **(Muito) obrigado** |
| | *(mweent) oh-bree**gah**-doo* |

| Don't mention it | **Não tem importância** |
| | *nowng tayng eempoor-**tanss**-yuh* |

| I'm sorry | **Desculpe** |
| | *dush**koolp*** |

| I'm on holiday here | **Estou aqui de férias** |
| | *shtoh a**kee** duh **fehr**-yush* |

| This is my first trip to … | **Esta é a minha primeira viagem a …** |
| | *esh**tuh** e uh **meen**-yuh pree**may**-ruh vee-**ah**-jayng uh …* |

| Do you mind if I smoke? | **Importa-se se eu fumar?** |
| | *eem**por**tuh-suh see ay-oo foo**mar*** |

| Would you like a drink? | **Quer uma bebida?** |
| | *kehr **oom**uh be**bee**duh* |

| Have you ever been to Britain? | **Já foi á Grã-Bretanha?** |
| | *ja foy a grambruh-**tahn**-yuh* |

| Did you like it there? | **Gostou de lá estar?** |
| | *goosh-**toh** duh la shtar* |

| What part of Portugal are you from? | **De que parte de Portugal é?** |
| | *duh kuh part duh poortoo-**gal** e* |

CONVERSION CHARTS

In the weight and length charts the middle figure can be either metric or imperial. Thus 3.3 feet = 1 metre, 1 foot = 0.3 metres, and so on.

feet		metres	inches		cm	lbs		kg
3.3	1	0.3	0.39	1	2.54	2.2	1	0.45
6.6	2	0.61	0.79	2	5.08	4.4	2	0.91
9.9	3	0.91	1.18	3	7.62	6.6	3	1.4
13.1	4	1.22	1.57	4	10.6	8.8	4	1.8
16.4	5	1.52	1.97	5	12.7	11	5	2.2
19.7	6	1.83	2.36	6	15.2	13.2	6	2.7
23	7	2.13	2.76	7	17.8	15.4	7	3.2
26.2	8	2.44	3.15	8	20.3	17.6	8	3.6
29.5	9	2.74	3.54	9	22.9	19.8	9	4.1
32.9	10	3.05	3.9	10	25.4	22	10	4.5
			4.3	11	27.9			
			4.7	12	30.1			

°C	0	5	10	15	17	20	22	24	26	28	30	35	37	38	40	50	100
°F	32	41	50	59	63	68	72	75	79	82	86	95	98.4	100	104	122	212

Km	10	20	30	40	50	60	70	80	90	100	110	120
Miles	6.2	12.4	18.6	24.9	31	37.3	43.5	49.7	56	62	68.3	74.6

Tyre pressures

lb/sq in	15	18	20	22	24	26	28	30	33	35
kg/sq cm	1.1	1.3	1.4	1.5	1.7	1.8	2	2.1	2.3	2.5

Liquids

gallons	1.1	2.2	3.3	4.4	5.5
litres	5	10	15	20	25

pints	0.44	0.88	1.76
litres	0.25	0.5	1

CUSTOMS & PASSPORTS

I have nothing to declare	**Não tenho nada a declarar** *nowng ten-yoo nah-duh uh duh-klarar*
I have the usual allowances of alcohol/tobacco	**Trago as quantidades de álcool/tabaco autorizadas** *trah-goo ush kwantee-dah-dush dalkoo-ol/ toobah-koo owtooree-zah-dush*
I have two bottles of wine to declare	**Tenho duas garrafas de vinho a declarar** *ten-yoo doo-ush garrah-fush duh veen-yoo uh duh-klarar*
My wife/My husband and I have a joint passport	**A minha mulher/O meu marido e eu temos um passaporte familiar** *uh meen-yuh mool-yehr/oo mayoo mareedoo ee ayoo tay-mooz oom passuh-port fameel-yar*
The children are on this passport	**As crianças estão neste passaporte** *ush kree-ansush shtowng naysht passuh-port*
I am a British national	**Eu sou de nacionalidade britânica** *ay-oo soh duh nas-yoonalee-dahd bree-tahnikuh*
I am here on business	**Estou aqui em viagem de negócios** *shtoh akee ayng vee-ah-jayng duh negoss-yoosh*
I have an entry visa	**Tenho um visto de entrada** *ten-yoo oom veeshtoo dayn-trah-duh*

What is the date today?	**A quantos estamos hoje?**	*uh **kwan**-toosh **shtah**-mooz ohj*
It's the …	**Hoje é dia …**	*ohj e dee-uh …*
1st of March	**1 de Março**	*preemay-roo duh **mar**soo*
2nd of June	**2 de Junho**	*doysh duh **joon**-yoo*
We will arrive on the 29th of August	**Chegamos no dia vinte e nove de Agosto**	*shuhgah-moosh noo **dee**-uh veent ee nov dagoshtoo*
1984	**mil novecentos e oitenta e quatro**	*meel nov-**sentooz** ee oytent ee **kwa**troo*
Monday	**segunda-feira**	*segoonduh-**fay**-ruh*
Tuesday	**terça-feira**	*tehr-suh-**fay**-ruh*
Wednesday	**quarta-feira**	*kwartuh-**fay**-ruh*
Thursday	**quinta-feira**	*keentuh-**fay**-ruh*
Friday	**sexta-feira**	*seshtuh-**fay**-ruh*
Saturday	**sábado**	***sa**badoo*
Sunday	**domingo**	*doo**meen**goo*
January	**Janeiro**	*ja**nay**-roo*
February	**Fevereiro**	*fuv-**ray**-roo*
March	**Março**	***mar**soo*
April	**Abril**	*a**breel***
May	**Maio**	***my**-oo*
June	**Junho**	***joon**-yoo*
July	**Julho**	***jool**-yoo*
August	**Agosto**	*a**gosh**too*
September	**Setembro**	*se**tem**broo*
October	**Outubro**	*oh-**too**broo*
November	**Novembro**	*noo**vem**broo*
December	**Dezembro**	*de**zem**broo*

See also **NUMBERS**

DENTIST

Streetwise

I need to see the dentist (urgently)

Preciso de ir ao dentista (urgentemente)
*pre-**see**zoo deer ow den-**teesh**tuh (oorjent-**ment**)*

I have toothache

Doem-me os dentes
***do**-ayng-muh oosh dentsh*

I've broken a tooth

Tenho um dente partido
***ten**-yoo oom dent par-**tee**doo*

A filling has come out

Caíu-me um chumbo
*ka**yoo**-muh oom **shoom**boo*

Please give me an injection

Por favor, dê-me uma injecção
*poor fa**vor** day-muh **oom**uh eenje-**sowng***

My dentures need repairing

A minha placa tem que ser arranjada
*uh **meen**-yuh **plah**-kuh tayng kuh sehr arran**jah**-duh*

THE DENTIST MAY SAY:

Tenho que lho tirar
ten**-yoo kuh l-yoo tee**rar

I shall have to take it out

Precisa de um chumbo
*pre-**see**zuh doom **shoom**boo*

You need a filling

Talvez lhe doa um pouco
*tal**vesh** l-yuh **doh**-uh oom **poh**-koo*

This might hurt a bit

30

Streetwise

Excuse me, how do I get to the airport?	**Desculpe, como se vai para o aeroporto?** *dush**koolp** koh-moo suh vy pro uh-ehroo-**por**too*
Where is the nearest post office?	**Onde fica a estação dos correios mais próxima?** *onduh **fee**kuh uh shta-**sowng** doosh koo-**ray**oosh mysh **pross**imuh*
Is this the right way to the cathedral?	**É este o caminho para a catedral?** *e aysht oo ka**meen**-yoo pra katuh-**dral***
I am looking for the tourist office	**Procuro o turismo** *proo**koo**roo oo too**reej**-moo*
Is it far to walk/by car?	**Fica muito longe para ir a pé/de carro?** *fee**kuh **mween**too lonj **p**aruh eer uh pe/ duh **kar**roo*
Which is the road to …?	**Qual a estrada que vai para …?** *kwal uh **shrah**-duh kuh vy **p**aruh …*
Is this the turning for …?	**É aqui que se vira para …?** *e a**kee** kuh suh **vee**ruh **p**aruh …*
How do I get onto the motorway?	**Como se vai para a autoestrada?** ***koh**-moo suh vy pra owtoo-**shtrah**-duh*
I have lost my way	**Perdi-me** *Per**dee**-muh*
Can you show me on the map?	**Pode mostrar-me no mapa?** *pod moosh**trar**-muh noo **mah**-puh*

DOCTOR

Streetwise

I need a doctor	**Preciso de ir ao médico** *pre-seezoo deer ow medikoo*
Can I make an appointment with the doctor?	**Posso ter uma consulta com o médico?** *possoo tehr oomuh konsooltuh kong oo medikoo*
My son/My wife is ill	**O meu filho/A minha mulher está doente** *oo mayoo feel-yoo/uh meen-yuh mool-yehr shta doo-ent*
I have a sore throat/ a stomach upset	**Dói-me a garganta/o estômago** *doy-muh uh gargantuh/oo shtoh-magoo*
He has diarrhoea/ earache	**Ele tem diarreia/dores de ouvidos** *ayl tayng dee-uh-rayuh/dorush doh-veedoosh*
I am constipated	**Tenho prisão de ventre** *ten-yoo preezowng duh ventruh*
I have a pain here/ in my chest	**Dói-me aqui/o peito** *doy-muh akee/oo paytoo*
He has been stung/ bitten	**Ele foi picado/mordido** *ayl foy peekah-doo/moordeedoo*
He can't breathe/walk	**Ele não pode respirar/andar** *ayl nowng pod rushpeerar/andar*
She has a temperature	**Ela tem febre** *eluh tayng februh*

I feel dizzy	**Sinto-me tonto** *seentoo-muh **tontoo***
I can't sleep/swallow	**Não posso dormir/engolir** *nowng **posso**o doormeer/ayngoo-**leer***
She has been sick	**Ela vomitou** *el*uh voomee**toh**
I am diabetic/I am pregnant	**Sou diabético/Estou grávida** *soh dee-uh-**bet**ikoo/shtoh **grav**iduh*
I am allergic to penicillin/cortisone	**Sou alérgico à penicilina/cortisona** *soh a**lehr**-jikoo a punneesee-**lee**nuh/ koortee-**zon**uh*
I have high blood pressure	**Tenho a tensão alta** *ten*-yoo uh tayn-**sowng al**tuh*
My blood group is A positive/O negative	**O meu grupo sanguíneo é A positivo/O negativo** *oo **may**oo **groo**poo san**geen**-yoo e a poozee-**tee**voo/oo nuh-guh-**tee**voo*

THE DOCTOR MAY SAY:

Tem que ficar na cama *tayng kuh fee**kar** nuh **kah**-muh*	You must stay in bed
Ele tem que ir para o hospital *ayl tayng kuh eer pro oshpee**tal***	He will have to go to hospital
Tem que ser operado *tayng kuh sehr oh-pe**rah**-doo*	You will need an operation
Tome isto três/quatro vezes por dia *tom **eesh**too traysh/**kwa**troo **vay**-zush poor **dee**-uh*	Take this three/four times a day

33

DRINKS

Streetwise

In a bar or a café you order first and pay when you leave – waiters always keep a note of items consumed. Tea is drunk far more than in most continental countries and is especially good in a tea shop (salão de chá). Coffee is usually drunk strong and black (uma bica in Lisbon, um café in other areas), but you can also have a large milky coffee (um galão) or a coffee with a little milk (um garoto). The best places for snacks are a pastelaria or a confeitaria (cake shops), or 'snack-bars' or cafés.

A black coffee/A white coffee, please	**Um café/Um café com leite, por favor** *oom kuh-fe/oom kuh-fe kong layt poor favor*
Two cups of tea	**Duas chávenas de chá** *doo-ush sha-venush duh sha*
A pot of tea	**Um chá** *oom sha*
A glass of lemonade	**Uma limonada** *oomuh leemoonah-duh*
A bottle of mineral water	**Uma garrafa de água mineral** *oomuh garraf-fuh dahg-wuh meenuh-ral*
Do you have …?	**Tem …?** *tayng …*
With ice, please	**Com gelo, por favor** *kong jayloo poor favor*
Another coffee, please	**Outro café, por favor** *oh-troo kuh-fe poor favor*

See also **WINES & SPIRITS**

Streetwise

Drive on the right-hand side of the road and remember that traffic coming from the right has priority. Speed limits are 50 km/h in urban areas, 90 km/h on ordinary roads and 120 km/h on motorways. Seat belts are compulsory on the open road, but not in urban areas. Portuguese drivers rarely respect zebra crossings, so mind your rear if you intend to stop at one! Be warned that wheel clamps are now used to punish illegal parking. Note also that it is obligatory to use your horn as a warning at bends on narrow, winding country roads.

What is the speed limit on this road?	**Qual é o limite de velocidade nesta estrada?** *kwal e oo leemeet duh veloo-seedahd neshtuh shtrah-duh*
Is there a toll on this motorway?	**Há portagem nesta autoestrada?** *a poortah-jayng neshtuh owtoo-shtrah-duh*
Is there a short cut?	**Há um atalho?** *a oom atal-yoo*
Where can I park?	**Onde posso estacionar?** *onduh possoo shtass-yoonar*
Is there a car park nearby?	**Há um parque de estacionamento perto?** *a oom park duh shtass-yoonuh-mentoo pehrtoo*
Can I park here?	**Posso estacionar aqui?** *possoo shtass-yoonar akee*
How long can I stay here?	**Quanto tempo posso ficar aqui?** *kwantoo tempoo possoo feekar akee*
Do I need a parking disc?	**Preciso de um disco de estacionamento?** *pre-seezoo doom deeshkoo duh shtass-yoonuh-mentoo*

See also **ACCIDENTS - CARS, BREAKDOWNS, PETROL STATION, POLICE**

Streetwise

Set-price menus are often good value. VAT (IVA) is normally included in prices. If you want a light meal, cake shops and tea houses offer savoury pastries and pies as well as delicious sweet buns and breads.

Is there a restaurant/café near here?
Há um restaurante/um café perto?
*a oom rushtoh-**rant**/oom kuh-**fe pehr**too*

A table for four, please
Uma mesa para quatro, por favor
*oomuh **may**-zuh paruh **kwat**roo poor fa**vor***

May we see the menu?
Pode-nos dar a ementa?
***pod**-noosh dar uh ee**men**tuh*

We'll take the set menu, please
Queremos a refeição da casa, por favor
***kray**-mooz uh ruh-fay-**sowng** duh **kah**zuh poor favor*

We'd like a drink first
Queremos uma bebida primeiro
***kray**-mooz **oom**uh be**bee**duh pree-**may**roo*

Could we have some more bread/water?
Pode trazer mais pão/água?
*pod tra**zehr** mysh powng/**ahg**-wuh*

We'd like a dessert/some mineral water
Queremos a sobremesa/água mineral
kray**-mooz uh sobruh-**may**zuh/**ahg**-wuh meenuh-**ral

The bill, please
A conta, por favor
*uh **kon**tuh poor favor*

Is service included?
O serviço está incluído?
*oo ser**vee**soo shta een-**klwee**doo*

Streetwise

There's a fire!	**Há fogo!** *a foh-goo*
Call a doctor/an ambulance!	**Chamem um médico/uma ambulância!** *shah-mayng oom medikoo/oomuh amboolanss-yuh*
We must get him to hospital	**Temos que o levar ao hospital** *tay-moosh kee oo levar ow oshpeetal*
Fetch help quickly!	**Procure ajuda depressa** *prookoor ajooduh depressuh*
Get the police!	**Chame a polícia!** *shahm uh pooleess-yuh*
Where's the nearest hospital?	**Onde fica o hospital mais próximo?** *onduh feekuh oo oshpeetal mysh pro-seemoo*
I've lost my credit card/my wallet	**Perdi o meu cartão de crédito/a minha carteira** *perdee oo mayoo kartowng duh kreditoo/uh meen-yuh kartay-ruh*
My child is missing	**Não encontro o meu filho** *nowng ayng-kontroo oo mayoo feel-yoo*
My passport has been stolen	**O meu passaporte foi roubado** *oo mayoo passuh-port foy roh-bah-doo*

See also **ACCIDENTS, BREAKDOWNS, DENTIST, DOCTOR**

ENTERTAINMENT

Streetwise

The traditional song of Portugal is the fado and there are special clubs called casas de fado where you can go to listen to this music while you dine. Most regions and towns have special carnival-like festivities (festas), mainly in spring and summer, so ask at tourist offices for details. On Portuguese television and in cinemas almost all films are shown in the original language.

Are there any local festivals?
Há algumas festas locais?
a algoomush feshtush lookysh

Can you recommend something for the children?
Pode recomendar alguma coisa para as crianças?
pod rekoomen-dar algoomuh koyzuh prash kree-ansush

What is there to do in the evenings?
O que é que há para fazer à noite?
oo kee e kee a paruh fazehr a noyt

Where is there a cinema/a theatre?
Onde é que há um cinema/um teatro?
ondee e kee a oom seenay-muh/oom tee-ah-troo

Where can we go to a concert?
Onde é que há um concerto?
ondee e kee a oom konsehr-too

Can you book the tickets for us?
Pode marcar-nos os bilhetes?
pod markar-nooz ooj beel-yetsh

Are there any night-clubs/discos?
Há algumas boites/discotecas?
a algoomush bwatsh/deeshkoo-tekush

Can we go fishing/riding?
Podemos pescar/andar a cavalo?
pooday-moosh pushkar/andar uh kavah-loo

Where can we play tennis/golf?
Onde podemos jogar ténis/golfe?
onduh pooday-moosh joogar tayneesh/golf

See also **NIGHTLIFE, SIGHTSEEING**

What time is the next sailing?	**A que horas parte o próximo barco?** *uh kee orush part oo prossimoo barkoo*
A return ticket for one car, two adults and two children	**Um bilhete de ida e volta para um carro, dois adultos e duas crianças** *oom beel-yet duh eeduh ee voltuh paruh oom karroo doyz adooltooz ee doo-ush kree-ansush*
How long does the crossing take?	**Quanto tempo demora a trevessia?** *kwantoo tempoo demoruh uh travuh-see-uh*
Are there any cabins/ reclining seats?	**Há camarotes/bancos reclináveis?** *a kamuh-rotsh/bankoosh ruh-kleenah-vaysh*
Is there a bar/TV lounge?	**Há um bar/uma sala de televisão?** *a oom bar/oomuh sah-luh duh tuh-luh-veezowng*
Where are the toilets?	**Onde fica a casa de banho?** *onduh feekuh uh kah-zuh duh bahn-yoo*
Where is the duty-free shop?	**Onde fica a loja franca?** *onduh feekuh uh lojuh frankuh*
Can we go out on deck?	**Podemos ir para o convés?** *pooday-mooz eer pro komvesh*
What is the sea like today?	**Como está o mar hoje?** *koh-moo shta oo mar ohj*

GIFTS & SOUVENIRS

Streetwise

Best buys are cork and linen goods, which, although expensive, are of excellent quality and craftsmanship. Pottery and ceramics are also a good buy and you'll find a wide variety of styles and shapes available, including many traditional designs.

Where can we buy souvenirs of the cathedral?	**Onde é que podemos comprar lembranças desta catedral?** *ondee e kuh pooday-moosh komprar laym-bransush deshtuh katuh-dral*
Where is the nearest gift shop?	**Onde fica a loja de lembranças mais próxima?** *onduh feekuh uh lojuh duh laym-bransush mysh prossimuh*
I want to buy a present for my husband/my wife	**Quero comprar um presente para o meu marido/a minha mulher** *kehroo komprar oom prezent pro mayoo mareedoo/uh meen-yuh mool-yehr*
What is the local/regional speciality?	**Qual é a especialidade local/regional?** *kwal e uh shpuss-yalee-dahd lookal/ruj-yoonal*
Is this hand-made?	**Isto é feito à mão?** *eeshtoo e faytoo a mowng*
Have you anything suitable for a young child?	**Tem alguma coisa para crianças?** *tayng algoomuh koy-zuh paruh kree-ansush*
I want something cheaper/more expensive	**Quero uma coisa mais barata/mais cara** *kehroo oomuh koy-zuh mysh barah-tuh/mysh kah-ruh*
Please wrap it up for me	**Por favor, embrulhe-me isso** *poor favor aymbrool-yuh-muh eesoo*

Nouns

Portuguese nouns are *masculine* or *feminine*, and their gender is shown by the words for 'the' and 'a' used before them (the 'article'):

masculine	*feminine*
o/um castelo the/a castle	**a/uma mesa** the/a table
os castelos/(uns) castelos	**as mesa/(umas) mesas**
the castles/castles	the tables/tables

It is usually possible to tell whether a noun is masculine or feminine by its ending: nouns ending in **-o** or **-or** are usually masculine, while those ending in **-a**, **-agem**, **-dade** and **-tude** tend to be feminine. There are exceptions, however, and it's best to learn the noun and the article together.

Plural

Nouns ending in a vowel form the plural by adding **-s**, while those ending in a consonant usually add **-es**. The exceptions to this are words ending in an **-m** which change to **-ns** in the plural and words ending in **-l** which change to **-is** in the plural: e.g. **hotel – hotéis**.

NOTE: When used after the words **a** (to), **de** (of), **em** (in) and **por** (by), the articles (and many other words) contract:

a + as = às *ash*	to the
de + um = dum *doom*	of a
em + uma = numa *noomuh*	to a
por + os = pelos *peloosh*	by the

'This', 'That', 'These', 'Those'

These depend on the gender and number of the noun they represent:

este menino	this boy	**esta menina**	this girl
estes meninos	these boys	**estas meninas**	these girls
esse menino	that boy	**essa menina**	that girl
esses meninos	those boys	**essas meninas**	those girls
aquele menino	that boy (over there)	**aquela menina**	that girl (over there)
aqueles meninos	those boys (over there)	**aquelas meninas**	those girls (over there)

GRAMMAR 2

Adjectives

Adjectives normally follow the nouns they describe in Portuguese, e.g. **a maçã verde** (the green apple). Some exceptions which precede the noun are:

muito much, many; **pouco** few; **tanto** so much, so many; **primeiro** first; **último** last; **bom** good; **nenhum** no, not any; **grande** great.

Portuguese adjectives have to reflect the gender of the noun they describe. To make an adjective feminine, **-o** endings change to **-a**, and **-or** and **-ês** change to **-ora** and **-esa**. Otherwise they generally have the same form for both genders. Thus:

masculine	*feminine*
o livro vermelho	**a saia vermelha**
(the red book)	(the red skirt)
o homem falador	**a mulher faladora**
(the talkative man)	(the talkative woman)

To make an adjective plural, follow the general rules given for nouns.

'My', 'Your', 'His', 'Her'

These words also depend on the gender and number of the following noun and not on the sex of the 'owner'.

	with masculine	*with feminine*	*with plural nouns*
my	**o meu**	**a minha**	**os meus/as minhas**
	mayoo	*meen-yuh*	*mayoosh/meen-yush*
his/her/its/your	**o seu** *sayoo*	**a sua** *soo-uh*	**os seus/as suas**
our	**o nosso** *nossoo*	**a nossa** *nossuh*	**os nossos/as nossas**
their/your	**o seu** *sayoo*	**a sua** *soo-uh*	**os seus/as suas**

NOTE: Since **o seu, a sua**, etc can mean 'his', 'her', 'your', etc, Portuguese will often replace them with the words for 'of him', 'of her', 'of you', etc (**dele, dela, de você**, etc) in order to avoid confusion:

os livros *dela*	her books
os livros *de você*	your books
os livros *deles*	their books

Pronouns

SUBJECT			OBJECT		
I	**eu**	*ay-oo*	me	**me**	*muh*
you	**você**	*voh-se*	you	**o/a**	*oo/uh*
he	**ele**	*ayl*	him	**o**	*oo*
she	**ela**	*eluh*	her	**a**	*uh*
it	**ele/ela**	*ayl/eluh*	it	**o/a**	*oo/uh*
we	**nós**	*nosh*	us	**nos**	*noosh*
you	**vocês**	*voh-sesh*	you	**os/as**	*oosh/ush*
they (masc.)	**eles**	*aylush*	them (masc.)	**os**	*oosh*
(fem.)	**elas**	*elush*	(fem.)	**as**	*ush*

NOTES

1. Subject pronouns are normally not used except for emphasis or to avoid confusion:

> *eu* **vou para Lisboa e** *ele* **vai para Coimbra**
> *I*'m going to Lisbon and *he*'s going to Coimbra

2. Object pronouns are usually placed after the verb and joined with a hyphen:

> **vejo-***o*   I see him

However, in sentences beginning with a 'question word' or a 'negative word' the pronoun goes in front of the verb:

> **quando** *o* **viu?**   when did you see him?
> **não** *o* **vi**   I did not see him

Also, in sentences beginning with 'that' and 'who', etc ('subordinate clauses') the pronoun precedes the verb:

> **sei que** *o* **viu**   I know that you saw him
> **o homem que** *o* **viu**   the man who saw him

3. **Me** also = to me and **nos** = to us, but **lhe** = to him/to her/to it/to you and **lhes** = to them/to you.

4. When two pronouns are used together they are often shortened. The verb will also change spelling if it ends in **-r**, **-s**, **-z** or a nasal sound:

dá-mo	(= dá + me + o)	he gives me it
dê-lho	(= dê + lhe + o)	give him it
fá-lo	(= faz + o)	he does it
dão-nos	(= dão + os *or* dão + nos)	they give them *or* they give us

5. The pronoun following a preposition has the same form as the subject pronoun, except for **mim** (me), and **si** (you).

Verbs

There are three main patterns of endings for verbs in Portuguese – those ending **-ar**, **-er** and **-ir** in the dictionary.

cantar	to sing	**comer**	to eat
canto	I sing	**como**	I eat
canta	he/she/it sings/you sing	**come**	he/she/it eats/you eat
cantamos	we sing	**comemos**	we eat
cantam	they/you sing	**comem**	they/you eat

partir	to leave
parto	I leave
parte	he/she/it leaves/you leave
partimos	we leave
partem	they/you leave

And in the past tense:

cantei	I sang	**comei**	I ate
cantou	he/she/it/you sang	**comeu**	he/she/it/you ate
cantámos	we sang	**comemos**	we ate
cantaram	they/you sang	**comeram**	they/you ate

parti	I left
partiu	he/she/it/you left
partimos	we left
partiram	they/you left

Four of the most common verbs are irregular:

ser	to be	**estar**	to be
sou	I am	**estou**	I am
é	he/she/it is/you are	**está**	he/she/it is/you are
somos	we are	**estamos**	we are
são	they/you are	**estão**	they/you are

ter	to have	**ir**	to go
tenho	I have	**vou**	I go
tem	he/she/it has/you have	**vai**	he/she/it goes/you go
temos	we have	**vamos**	we go
têm	they/you have	**vão**	they/you go

GREETINGS

Streetwise

Portuguese has two forms of address, formal and informal. If you know someone very well you say tu. The formal greeting is o senhor for gentlemen and a senhora for ladies. In Portugal you shake hands on meeting and on saying goodbye.

Hello	**Olá** *oh-la*
Good morning/Good afternoon/Good evening	**Bom dia/Boa tarde/Boa noite** *bong dee-uh/boh-uh tard/boh-uh noyt*
Goodbye	**Adeus** *aday-oosh*
Good night	**Boa noite** *boh-uh noyt*
How do you do?	**Como está?** *koh-moo shta*
Pleased to meet you?	**Prazer em conhecê-lo** *prazehr ayng koon-yuh-seh-loo*
How are you?	**Como está?** *koh-moo shta*
Fine, thank you	**Bem obrigado** *bayng oh-breegah-doo*
See you soon	**Até breve** *ate brev*
See you later	**Até logo** *ate logoo*

I'd like to make an appointment	**Queria marcar a vez** *kree-uh markar uh vesh*
A cut and blow-dry, please	**Cortar e secar, por favor** *koortar ee sekar poor favor*
A shampoo and set	**Lavar e fazer mise** *lavar ee fazehr meez*
Not too short	**Não muito curto** *nowng mweentoo koortoo*
I'd like it layered	**Queria o cabelo cortado em dégradé** *kree-uh oo kabay-loo koortah-doo ayng day-graday*
Not too much off the back/fringe	**Não corte muito atrás/a franja** *nowng kort mweentoo atrash/uh franjuh*
Take more off the top/the sides	**Corte mais por cima/dos lados** *kort mysh poor seemuh/doosh lah-doosh*
My hair is permed/tinted	**Tenho uma permanente/o cabelo pintado** *ten-yoo oomuh permuh-nent/oo kabay-loo peentah-doo*
My hair is naturally curly/straight	**O meu cabelo é encaracolado/liso** *oo mayoo kabay-loo e ayng-karahkoo-lah-doo/leezoo*
It's too hot	**Está quente demais** *shta kent duh-mysh*
I'd like a conditioner/some hair spray	**Queria creme amaciador/laca** *kree-uh krem amuss-yuh-dor/lah-kuh*

HOTEL DESK

Streetwise

I have reserved a room
in the name of …

Reservei um quarto em nome de …
ruh-zervay oom kwartoo ayng nom duh …

I confirmed my
booking by phone/
by letter

**Confirmei a minha reserva pelo
telefone/por carta**
*komfeermay uh meen-yuh ruh-zehrvuh ploo
tuh-luh-fon/poor kartuh*

Could you have my
luggage taken up?

**Podem levar a minha bagagem para o
quarto?**
*podayng levar uh meen-yuh bagah-jayng pro
kwartoo*

What time is
breakfast/dinner?

**A que horas é o pequeno almoço/o
jantar?**
*uh kee oruz e oo puh-kay-noo almoh-soo/
oo jantar*

Please call me at …

Por favor, acorde-me às … (*see* TIME)
poor favor akord-muh ash …

I want to stay an
extra night

Quero ficar mais uma noite
kehroo feekar myz oomuh noyt

I shall be leaving
tomorrow morning

Parto amanhã de manhã
partoo aman-yang duh man-yang

See also **ACCOMMODATION, PAYING, ROOM SERVICE**

Streetwise

Main railway and bus stations, as well as airports, normally have a
left-luggage office (consigna). Porters will be found in railway stations
and airports, though not in bus stations.

Where do I check in
my luggage?

Onde faço o check-in?
onduh fah-soo oo check-in

Where is the luggage
from the Lisbon
flight/train?

**Onde está a bagagem do voo/do comboio
de Lisboa?**
*onduh shta uh bagah-jayng doo voh-oo/
doo komboyoo duh leej-boh-uh*

Our luggage has not
arrived

A nossa bagagem não chegou
uh nossuh bagah-jayng nowng shuh-goh

My suitcase was
damaged in transit

A minha mala estragou-se na viagem
*uh meen-yuh mah-luh shtragoh-suh nuh
vee-ah-jayng*

Where is the left-
luggage office?

Onde fica o depósito de bagagem?
onduh feekuh oo duh-pozitoo duh bagah-jayng

Are there any
luggage trolleys?

Há carrinhos para as bagagens?
a kareen-yoosh prash bagah-jaynsh

It's very heavy

É muito pesada
e mweentoo puh-zah-duh

Can you help me
with my bags?

Pode ajudar-me a levar os meus sacos?
*pod ajoodar-muh uh luh-var ooj mayoosh
sah-koosh*

Take my bag to a
taxi

Leve o meu saco para um táxi
lev oo mayoo sah-koo proom taxee

MAPS & GUIDES

The local tourist office may provide some basic maps and leaflets free of charge. Otherwise, you can buy maps in bookshops and at newspaper kiosks.

Where can I buy a local map?
Onde posso comprar um mapa local?
*onduh **possoo** kom**prar** oom **mah**-puh loo**kal***

Have you got a town plan?
Tem um mapa da cidade?
*tayng oom **mah**-puh duh see**dahd***

I want a street map of the city
Quero um mapa com as ruas da cidade
keh**roo oom **mah**-puh kong ush **roo**-ush duh see**dahd

I need a road map of ...
Preciso de um mapa das estradas de ...
*pre-**see**zoo doom **mah**-puh dush **shtrah**-dush duh ...*

Can I get a map at the tourist office?
Posso arranjar um mapa no turismo?
***possoo** arran**jar** oom **mah**-puh noo too**reej**-moo*

Can you show me on the map?
Pode-me mostrar no mapa?
***pod**-muh moosh**trar** noo **mah**-puh*

Do you have a guidebook in English?
Tem um guia turístico em inglês?
*tayng oom **ghee**-uh too**reesh**-tikoo ayng een**glesh***

Do you have a guidebook to the cathedral?
Tem um folheto desta catedral?
*tayng oom fool-**yet**oo **desh**tuh katuh-**dral***

See also **DIRECTIONS**

MEASUREMENTS

a litre of …
um litro de …
*oom **lee**troo duh …*

a kilo of …
um quilo di …
*oom **kee**loo duh …*

100 grammes of …
cem gramas de …
*sayng **grah**-mush duh …*

half a kilo of …
meio quilo de …
*mayoo **kee**loo duh …*

a half-bottle of …
meia garrafa de …
mayuh garraf-fuh duh …

a slice of …
uma fatia de …
oomuh fatee-uh duh …

a portion of …
um bocado de …
*oom boo**kah**-doo duh …*

a dozen …
uma dúzia de …
*oomuh **doo**zee-uh duh …*

1000 escudos worth (of) …
mil escudos de …
*meel **shkoo**doosh duh …*

a third
um terço
*oom **tehr**-soo*

two thirds
dos terços
*doysh **tehr**-soosh*

a quarter
um quarto
*oom **kwar**too*

three quarters
três quartos
*traysh **kwar**toosh*

ten per cent
dez por cento
*desh poor **sen**too*

more …
mais …
mysh …

less …
menos …
may-noosh …

enough …
bastante …
*bash-**tant** …*

double
o dobro
*oo **doh**-broo*

twice
duas vezes
*doo-ush **vay**-zush*

three times
três vezes
*traysh **vay**-zush*

See also **BUYING, NUMBERS, PAYING**

Portuguese cuisine varies a great deal from region to region with each area having its own speciality. For example, on the coast and in southern areas fish forms the main part of the diet while in the north and in the mountains there is greater dependence on meat, especially pork. Meal times can also vary according to the region or the season. A rough guide is as follows:

o pequeno almoço	(breakfast)	until 1000
o almoço	(lunch)	from noon until 1500
o jantar	(dinner)	from 1930 to 2200

Lunch tends to be the main meal of the day and is largely a choice between meat or fish dishes as in Britain, though each region has its own variations. Some typical Portuguese dishes worth trying include: *caldo verde* (cabbage soup); any of the seafood dishes for the main course; and *pudim flan/pudim molotov* (egg caramels) for dessert. A typical Portuguese menu is divided into the following sections:

Sopas	Soups
Peixes	Fish dishes
Mariscos	Seafood dishes
Carnes	Meat dishes
Ovos	Egg dishes
Sobremesas	Desserts
Queijos	Cheese

How is this dish served/cooked?	**Como é servido/preparado este prato?** *koh-moo e servee-doo/pruh-parah-doo aysht prah-too*
What is the chef's/ the house speciality?	**Qual é a especialidade do chefe/da casa?** *kwal e uh shpuss-yalee-dahd doo shef/duh kah-zuh*
What kind of seafood/ vegetables/fruit do you have?	**Que tipos de marisco/legumes/fruta tem?** *kuh teepoosh dih muh-reesh-koo/luh-goomsh/ frootuh tayng*

See also **EATING OUT, ORDERING, WINES & SPIRITS**

Streetwise

*The Portuguese currency is the escudo, which is divided into 100 centavos. The symbol for the escudo is the dollar sign ($). Coins come in denominations of 1, 2.5, 5, 10, 20, 25, 50, 100 and 200 escudos and you will find notes of 500, 1000, 5000, 10, 000 escudos. One thousand escudos is usually called a conto and this may even appear on some price tickets. For opening hours of banks and 'bureau de change', see **BUSINESS**. It is best to use banks for changing money, etc as commission rates are higher elsewhere. In most banks you carry out the transaction at one counter and then receive your money from the cashier (caixa). You will normally have to show your passport.*

I haven't enough money	**Não tenho dinheiro suficiente** *nowng **ten**-yoo deen-**yay**-roo soofeess-**yent***
Have you any change?	**Tem troco?** *tayng **tro**koo*
Can you change a 100-escudo note?	**Pode-me trocar cem escudos?** ***pod**-muh troo**kar** sayng **shkoo**doosh*
I'd like to change these traveller's cheques	**Quero trocar estes traveller cheques** ***kehr**oo troo**kar** **aysh**-tush traveller sheksh*
I want to change some escudos into pounds	**Quero cambiar escudos em libras** ***kehr**oo kamb-**yar** **shkoo**dooz ayng **lee**brush*
What is the rate for sterling/dollars?	**Qual é o câmbio da libra/do dólar** *kwal e oo **kamb**-yoo duh **lee**bruh/doo dollar*
I'd like to cash a cheque with my Eurocheque card	**Quero levantar um cheque com o meu cartão Eurocheque** ***kehr**oo luh-van**tar** oom shek kong oo **may**oo kar**towng** ay-ooroo**shek***

NIGHTLIFE

Streetwise

Entrance fees at discos and nightclubs usually include the cost of your first drink.

What is there to do in the evenings?	**O que há para fazer à noite?** *oo kee a **pa**ruh fa**zehr** a noyt*
Where can we go to see a cabaret?	**Onde é que há um espectáculo de variedades?** *ondee e kee a oom shpe-**tak**ooloo duh varee-uh-**dah**-dush*
Are there any good nightclubs/good discos?	**Há algumas boites boas/discotecas boas?** *a al**goo**mush bwatsh **boh**-ush/deeshkoo-**tek**ush **boh**-ush*
Do we need to be members?	**Precisamos de ser sócios?** *pre-see**zah**-moosh duh sehr **soss**-yoosh*
How much does it cost to get in?	**Quanto custa o bilhete de entrada?** ***kwan**too **koosh**tuh oo beel-**yet** dayn-**trah**-duh*
We'd like to reserve two seats for tonight	**Queremos reservar dois lugares para esta noite** ***kray**-moosh ruh-zer**var** doysh loo**gar**ush **pa**ruh **esh**tuh noyt*
Is there a bar/a restaurant?	**Há um bar/um restaurante?** *a oom bar/oom rushtoh-**rant***
What time does the show/concert begin?	**A que horas começa o espectáculo/o concerto?** *uh kee **or**ush koo**mess**uh oo shpe-**tak**ooloo/ oo kon**sehr**-too*
Which film is on at the cinema?	**Que filme está hoje no cinema?** *kuh feelm shta ohj noo see**nay**-muh*

See also **EATING OUT, ENTERTAINMENT**

0	zero *zehr-oo*	13	treze *trayz*	50	cinquenta *seenkwentuh*
1	um *oom*	14	catorze *katorz*	60	sessenta *sesentuh*
2	dois *doysh*	15	quinze *keenz*	70	setenta *setentuh*
3	três *traysh*	16	dezasseis *dezuh-saysh*	80	oitenta *oytentuh*
4	quatro *kwatroo*	17	dezassete *dezuh-set*	90	noventa *nooventuh*
5	cinco *seenkoo*	18	dezoito *dezoytoo*	100	cem *sayng*
6	seis *saysh*	19	dezanove *dezuh-nov*	110	cento e dez *sentoo ee desh*
7	sete *set*	20	vinte *veent*	200	duzentos *doozentoosh*
8	oito *oytoo*	21	vinte e um *veentee-oom*	300	trezentos *trezentoosh*
9	nove *nov*	22	vinte e dois *veentee-doysh*	500	quinhentos *keen-yentoosh*
10	dez *desh*	23	vinte e três *veentee-traysh*	1,000	mil *meel*
11	onze *onz*	30	trinta *treentuh*	2,000	dois mil *doysh meel*
12	doze *dohz*	40	quarenta *kwarentuh*	1,000,000	um milhão *oom meel-yowng*

1st	primeiro *preemayroo*	5th	quinto *keentoo*	9th	nono *noh-noo*
2nd	segundo *segoondoo*	6th	sexto *sesh-too*	10th	décimo *dessimoo*
3rd	terceiro *tersayroo*	7th	sétimo *setimoo*		
4th	quarto *kwartoo*	8th	oitavo *oytah-voo*		

See also **MEASUREMENTS**

ORDERING

Do you have a set menu?

Tem o prato do dia?
*tayng oo **prah**-too doo **dee**-uh*

We will have the menu at ... escudos

Queremos a ementa de ... (*see* NUMBERS) **escudos**
***kray**-mooz uh ee**men**tuh duh ... **shkoo**doosh*

May we see the wine list?

Pode-nos mostrar a lista de vinhos?
***pod**-noosh moosh**trar** uh **leesh**tuh duh **veen**-yoosh*

What do you recommend?

O que recomenda?
*oo kuh ruh-koo**men**duh*

Is there a local speciality?

Há alguma especialidade local?
*a al**goo**muh shpuss-yalee-**dahd** loo**kal***

How is this dish served?

Como é servido este prato?
***koh**-moo e ser**vee**doo aysht **prah**-too*

What is in this dish?

O que é que leva este prato?
*oo kee e kuh **lev**uh aysht **prah**-too*

Are the vegetables included?

Também tem legumes?
*tam**bayng** tayng luh-**goomsh***

Rare/medium rare/ well done, please

Mal passado/médio/bem passado, por favor
*mal pa**sah**-doo/**med**-yoo/bayng pa**sah**-doo poor fa**vor***

We'd like a dessert/ some coffee, please

Queremos a sobremesa/café, por favor
kray**-mooz uh sobruh-**may**zuh/kuh-**fe** poor fa**vor

See also EATING OUT, MENUS, PAYING, WINES & SPIRITS

Streetwise

Credit cards, especially VISA and American Express, are accepted in most large hotels, restaurants and shops. Traveller's cheques and Eurocheques are also accepted (look for the sign on the door). Some petrol stations will only take cash. VAT (IVA) is included unless otherwise stated, as are service charges.

Can I have the bill, please?	**Pode trazer a conta, por favor?** *pod trazehr uh kontuh poor favor*
Is service/tax included?	**O serviço/imposto está incluído?** *oo serveesoo/eemposhtoo shta een-klweedoo*
What does that come to?	**Qual é o total?** *kwal e oo tootal*
How much is that?	**Quanto custa aquilo?** *kwantoo kooshtuh akeeloo*
Do I pay a deposit?	**Deixo depósito?** *day-shoo duh-pozitoo*
Can I pay by credit card/cheque?	**Posso pagar com o cartão de crédito/um cheque?** *possoo pagar kong oo kartowng duh kreditoo/ oom shek*
Do you accept traveller's cheques?	**Aceita traveller cheques?** *asaytuh traveller sheksh*
I'd like a receipt, please	**Quero um recibo, por favor** *kehroo oom ruh-seeboo poor favor*
Can I have an itemized bill?	**Pode-me dar uma factura com os artigos discriminados?** *pod-muh dar oomuh fak-tooruh kong ooz artee-goosh deesh-kreemee-nah-doosh*

See also **BUYING, MONEY**

Streetwise

You should carry your passport at all times, in case you are asked to show identification to the police.

My name is …	**Chamo-me …** *shah-moo-muh …*
My date of birth is …	**Nasci no dia …** *nash-see noo dee-uh …*
My address is …	**A minha morada é …** *uh meen-yuh moorah-duh e …*
I come from Britain/America	**Sou britânico/americano** *soh bree-tahnikoo/ameree-kah-noo*
I live in …	**Moro em …** *moh-roo ayng …*
My passport/My driving licence number is …	**O número do meu passaporte/da minha carta de condução é …** *oo noomeroo doo mayoo passuh-port/duh meen-yuh kartuh duh kondoo-sowng e …*
My blood group is …	**O meu grupo sanguíneo é …** *oo mayoo groopoo sangeen-yoo e …*
I work in an office/a factory	**Trabalho num escritório/numa fábrica** *trabal-yoo noom shkreetor-yoo/noomuh*
I am a secretary/manager	**Sou secretária/gerente** *soh sekruh-tar-yuh/juh-rent*
I'm here on holiday/on business	**Estou aqui de férias/em negócios** *shtoh akee duh fehr-yush/ayng negoss-yoosh*

Streetwise

Petrol stations are sometimes hard to locate – often they are just a pump on the pavement – so you have to look carefully to find one. There will be some familiar signs, but look especially for the green GALP sign, symbol of the national petrol company. Grades are super **** (four-star) and normal ** (two-star); diesel is gasóleo. Lead-free petrol (sem chumbo) has become more widespread. Few stations are open late or on Sundays so fill up while you can.

20 litres of two-star	**Vinte litros de gasolina normal** *veent **lee**troosh duh gazoo-**lee**nuh noor**mal***
3000 escudos (worth) of four-star petrol	**Três mil escudos de gasolina super** *traysh meel **shkoo**doosh duh gazoo-**lee**nuh **soo**per*
Fill it up, please	**Encha o depósito, por favor** *en**shuh** oo duh-**poz**itoo poor fa**vor***
Check the oil/the water	**Veja o óleo/a água** *ve**juh** oo **ol**-yoo/uh **ahg**-wuh*
Top up the wind-screen washers	**Veja a água do depósito do limpa pára-brisas** *ve**juh** uh **ahg**-wuh doo duh-**poz**itoo doo **leem**puh paruh-**bree**zush*
Could you clean the windscreen?	**Pode limpar o pára-brisas?** *pod leem**par** oo paruh-**bree**zush*
A can of oil, please	**Uma lata de óleo, por favor** *oo**muh** **lah**-tuh **dol**-yoo poor fa**vor***
Is there a telephone/ a lavatory?	**Há um telefone/uma casa de banho?** *a oom tuh-luh-**fon**/oo**muh** **kah**-zuh duh **bahn**-yoo*
I'd like my car washed	**Gostaria que me lavassem o carro** *gooshtuh-**ree**-uh kuh muh la**vass**ayng oo **karr**oo*

See also **DRIVING, PAYING**

PHOTOGRAPHY

Streetwise

Chemists' in Portugal do not sell photographic equipment or develop films as they do in Britain. Instead you must take your films to a specialist photographic shop. This is expensive though, so buy your films in Britain and have them developed at home. Taking photos in museums, galleries, etc is nearly always forbidden.

I need a colour/black and white film
Preciso de um rolo de fotografias a cores/a preto e branco
pre-seezoo doom roh-loo duh footoogruh-fee-ush uh korush/uh praytoo ee brankoo

It is for prints/slides
É para fotografias/slides
e paruh footoogruh-fee-ush/slydsh

There's something wrong with my camera
Tenho problemas com a minha máquina
ten-yoo proo-blemush kong uh meen-yuh makinuh

The film/The shutter has jammed
O filme/O obturador está preso
oo feelm/oo obtooruh-dor shta pray-zoo

The rewind mechanism does not work
A alavanca de rebobinagem não trabalha
uh aluh-vankuh duh ruh-boobee-nah-jayng nowng trabal-yuh

Can you develop this film?
Pode-me revelar este filme?
pod-muh ruh-vuh-lar aysht feelm

When will the photos be ready?
Quando é que as fotografias estão prontas?
kwandoo e kee ush footoogruh-fee-ush shtowng prontsh

Can I take photos in here?
Posso tirar fotografias aqui?
possoo teerar footoogruh-fee-uz akee

Streetwise

Police in Portugal can impose fines for traffic offences. The fine must be paid within 15 days at a police station, bank or post office.

We should call the police

Devemos chamar a polícia
*duh-**vay**-moosh sha**mar** uh poo**lees**-yuh*

Where is the police station?

Onde fica a esquadra?
*onduh **fee**kuh uh **shkwa**druh*

My car has been broken into

Assaltaram-me o carro
*assal-**tah**-rowng-muh oo **karr**oo*

I've been robbed

Fui roubado
*fwee roh-**bah**-doo*

I have had an accident

Tive um acidente
*teev oom asee**dent***

How much is the fine?

Quanto é a multa?
***kwan**too e uh **mool**tuh*

Can I pay at the police station?

Posso pagar na esquadra?
***poss**oo pagar nuh **shkwa**druh*

I don't have my driving licence on me

Não tenho aqui a minha carta de condução
*nowng **ten**-yoo a**kee** uh **meen**-yuh **kart**uh duh kondoo-**sowng***

I'm very sorry, officer

Lamento muito, senhor guarda
*lamen**too** mween**too** sun-**yor** **gward**uh*

I didn't know the regulations

Não conhecia as regras de trânsito
*nowng koon-yuh-**see**-uh ush **reg**rush duh **tran**zeetoo*

See also **ACCIDENTS, CUSTOMS & PASSPORTS, EMERGENCIES**

POST OFFICE

Streetwise

If you only want stamps, it's simplest to get them in a tobacconist's (tabacaria) or at shops displaying the 'selos' sign. Portuguese post offices (look for the CTT sign) are normally open 0900-1900. They have separate counters for different services, e.g. 'selos' for stamps and 'encomendas' for parcels. Letters take about five days on average to reach the UK. You will also find public telephones at post offices.

How much is a letter to England/America?	**Quanto custa mandar uma carta para a Inglaterra/a América?** *kwantoo kooshtouh mandar oomuh kartuh pra eengluh-terruh/amerikuh*
I'd like stamps for six postcards to Great Britain, please	**Quero selos para seis postais para a Grã-Bretanha, por favor** *kehroo seloosh paruh saysh poosh-tysh pra grambruh-tahn-yuh poor favor*
Twelve …-escudo stamps, please	**Doze selos de … escudos, por favor** *dohz seloosh duh … shkoodoosh poor favor*
I want to send a telegram to …	**Quero mandar um telegrama para …** *kehroo mandar oom tuh-luh-grah-muh paruh …*
When will it arrive?	**Quando é que chega?** *kwandoo e kuh shay-guh*
How much will it cost?	**Quanto custa?** *kwantoo kooshtuh*
Do I have to fill in a form?	**Tenho que preencher um impresso?** *ten-yoo kuh pree-enshehr oom eempressoo*
I'd like to make a telephone call	**Quero fazer uma chamada** *kehroo fazehr oomuh shamah-duh*

See also **TELEPHONE**

Can you help me, please?	**Pode-me ajudar, por favor?** *pod-muh ajoodar poor favor*
What is the matter?	**Qual é o problema?** *kwal e oo prooblemuh*
I am in trouble	**Tenho problemas** *ten-yoo prooblemush*
I don't understand	**Não compreendo** *nowng kompree-endoo*
Do you speak English?	**Fala inglês?** *fah-luh eenglesh*
Please repeat that	**Pode repetir isso, por favor?** *pod ruh-puh-teer eesoo poor favor*
I have run out of money	**Fiquei sem dinheiro** *feekay sayng deen-yay-roo*
My son is lost	**O meu filho perdeu-se** *oo mayoo feel-yoo perday-oo-suh*
I have lost my way	**Perdi-me** *perdee-muh*
I have forgotten my passport	**Esqueci-me do passaporte** *shkuh-see-muh doo passuh-port*
Please give me my passport back	**Por favor, devolva-me o passaporte** *poor favor duh-volvuh-muh oo passuh-port*
Where is the British Consulate?	**Onde fica o Consulado Britânico?** *onduh feekuh oo konsoo-lah-doo bree-tahnikoo*

See also **ACCIDENTS, COMPLAINTS, EMERGENCIES, POLICE**

PRONUNCIATION

In the pronunciation system used in this book, Portuguese sounds are represented by spellings of the nearest possible sound in English. Hence, when you read out the pronunciation – the line in italics after each phrase or word – sound the letters as if you were reading an English word. The syllable to be stressed is shown in **bold italics**. The following notes should help you:

	REMARKS	EXAMPLE	PRONOUNCED
a, e, o	as in pat, pet, pot	**pá, pé, pó**	*pa, pe, po*
ah, oh	as in ma, so	**maço, dou**	*mah-soo, doh*
ee, oo	as in tree, too	**triste, tudo**	*treesht, toodoo*
ay	as in may	**medo**	*may-doo*
eh	as in air	**aéreo**	*uh-ehr-yoo*
uh	as in mother	**que**	*kuh*
j	like s in leisure	**jejum**	*juh-joong*

There are a number of nasal sounds in Portuguese which, as with similar sounds in French, are pronounced by letting air out through the nose as well as the mouth:

	REMARKS	EXAMPLE	PRONOUNCED
ang	as in angry	**maçã**	*masang*
ayng	like mine	**mãe**	*myng*
ayng	like main	**homem**	*omayng*
eeng	midway between mean and Ming	**mim**	*meeng*
ong	as in Hong Kong	**com**	*kong*
oong	midway between goon and gong	**algum**	*al-goong*
owng	like town	**tão**	*towng*
oyng	like oi in point	**põe**	*poyng*

Pronouncing Portuguese words from their spelling is not easy as it is a 'flowing' language in which the sounds change depending on the way in which words are joined together. The following rules will help:

	REMARKS	EXAMPLE	PRONOUNCED
ç	as in facile	**faço**	*fah-soo*
ch	as in shampoo	**champô**	*shampoh*
h	always silent	**homem**	*omayng*
lh	like lli in million	**milhão**	*meel-yowng*
nh	like ni in opinion	**pinha**	*peen-yuh*

Streetwise

National Saints' days are public holidays. Each city and large town also has its own municipal holidays. Precise details will be available at the local tourist office.

New Year's Day	January 1st
Good Friday	
Freedom Day	April 25th
Labour Day	May 1st
Portuguese National Holiday	June 10th
Corpus Christi	June 21st
Assumption	August 15th
Republic Day	October 5th
All Saints' Day	November 1st
Restoration of Independence	December 1st
Immaculate Conception	December 8th
Christmas Day	December 25th

Streetwise

On main routes it is a good idea to reserve your seat in advance. For overnight travel you can book a sleeper or a couchette. Children under four travel free while those between four and 12 years old pay half fare. There is a 50% reduction for OAPs on journeys of over 50 km. The fastest trains are called rápidos, *while normal inter-city trains are called* intercidades.*

What time are the trains to …?	**A que horas partem os comboios para …?** *uh kee orush partayng oosh komboyoosh paruh …*
When is the next train to …?	**A que horas parte o próximo comboio para …?** *uh kee orush part oo prossimoo komboyoo paruh …*
What time does it arrive?	**A que horas chega?** *uh kee orush shay-guh*
Do I have to change?	**Tenho que mudar de comboio?** *ten-yoo kuh moodar duh komboyoo*
A first-/second-class single to …	**Um bilhete de primeira/segunda classe para …** *oom beel-yet duh preemay-ruh/segoonduh klass paruh …*
A return to …	**Um bilhete de ida e volta para …** *oom beelyet duh eeduh ee voltuh paruh …*
Is there a supplement to pay?	**É preciso pagar um suplemento?** *e pre-seezoo pagar oom soopluh-mentoo*
I want to reserve a sleeper	**Quero reservar uma carruagem-cama** *kehroo ruh-zervar oomuh kar-wah-jayng-kahmuh*

See also **LUGGAGE, TRAIN TRAVEL**

I have broken a glass/ the window	**Parti um vidro/a janela** *par**tee** oom **vee**droo/uh janeluh*
I have a hole in my shoe/these trousers	**Tenho um buraco no sapato/nestas calças** *ten-yoo oom boo**rah**-koo noo sa**pah**-too/ neshtush **kal**sush*
This is broken/torn	**Isto está partido/roto** *eeshtoo shta par**tee**doo/**roh**-too*
Can you repair this?	**Pode arranjar isto?** *pod arran**jar** eeshtoo*
Can you do it quickly?	**Pode fazê-lo com urgência?** *pod fa**zeh**-loo kong oor-**jenss**-yuh*
When can you get it done by?	**Quando é que está pronto?** ***kwan**doo e kuh shta pront*
I need some adhesive tape/a safety pin	**Preciso de fita adhesiva/de um alfinete de dama** *pre-**see**zoo duh **fee**tuh aduh-**zee**vuh/doom alfee**net** duh **dah**-muh*
The stitching has come undone	**Caíu-me uma malha** *ka**yoo**-muh **oom**uh **mal**-yuh*
Can you reheel these shoes?	**Pode pôr uns saltos nestes sapatos?** *pod por oonsh **sal**-toosh **naysh**-tush sa**pah**-toosh*
The door handle has come off	**O puxador da porta saiu** *oo pooshuh-**dor** duh **por**tuh sa-**yoo***

ROAD CONDITIONS

Streetwise

> Motorways are very good, but you usually have to pay a toll. 'A' roads are also fairly good in general but have only single-lane traffic and a slow vehicle lane on steep hills for overtaking. Minor roads are not always good, but they have the advantage of having very little heavy traffic. In mountain ranges in winter, snow chains are compulsory.

Is there a route that avoids the traffic?	**Há outra estrada para evitar o trânsito?** *a **oh**-truh **shtrah**-duh paruh eevee**tar** oo **tran**zeetoo*
Is the traffic heavy on the motorway?	**Há muito trânsito na autoestrada?** *a **mween**too **tran**zeetoo nuh owtoo-**shtrah**-duh*
What is causing this hold-up?	**Qual é a causa desta demora?** *kwal e uh **kow**zuh **desh**tuh duh-**mor**uh*
When will the road be clear?	**Quando é que a estrada vai ficar livre?** *kwan**doo** e kee uh **shtrah**-duh vy fee**kar** **leev**ruh*
Is there a detour?	**Há um desvio?** *a oom duj-**vee**-oo*
Is the road to … snowed up?	**A estrada para … está cheia de neve?** *uh **shtrah**-duh paruh … shta **shay**uh duh nev*
Is the pass/tunnel open?	**A passagem/O túnel está livre?** *uh pa**sah**-jayng/oo **too**nel shta **leev**ruh*
Do I need chains?	**Preciso de correntes?** *pre-**see**zoo duh koo**rentsh***

See also **DRIVING**, **WEATHER**

Come in!	**Entre!** *entruh*
We'd like breakfast/a bottle of wine in our room	**Queremos o pequeno almoço/uma garrafa de vinho no nosso quarto** *kray-mooz oo puh-kaynoo almoh-soo/oomuh garrah-fuh duh veen-yoo noo nossoo kwartoo*
Put it on my bill	**Ponha na minha conta** *pon-yuh nuh meen-yuh kontuh*
I'd like an outside line, please	**Quero uma chamada para o exterior, por favor** *kehroo oomuh shamah-duh pro shtuh-ree-or poor favor*
I have lost my key	**Perdi a minha chave** *perdee uh meen-yuh shahv*
I have locked myself out of my room	**Deixei a chave no meu quarto** *day-shay uh shahv noo mayoo kwartoo*
May I have an extra blanket/pillow?	**Pode-me dar mais um cobertor/uma almofada?** *pod-muh dar myz oom koobertor/oomuh almoofah-duh*
The TV/The radio does not work	**A televisão/O radio não trabalha** *uh tuh-luh-veezowng/oo rahd-yoo nowng trabal-yuh*
Please send someone to collect my luggage	**Por favor, mande alguém para levar a minha bagagem** *poor favor mand algayng paruh levar uh meen-yuh bagah-jayng*

See also **CLEANING, COMPLAINTS, HOTEL DESK, TELEPHONE**

SELF-CATERING

We've booked an apartment in the name of …

Reservámos um apartamento em nome de …
ruh-zer-vamooz oom apartuh-mentoo ayng nom duh …

Which is the key for the front door?

Qual é a chave da porta da frente?
kwal e uh shahv duh portuh duh frent

Please show us around

Por favor, mostre-nos a apartamento
poor favor moshtruh-nooz oo apartuh-mentoo

Where is the electricity meter/the water heater?

Onde está o contador da electricidade/o esquentador?
onduh shta oo kontuh-dor duh eeletree-seedahd/ oo shkentuh-dor

How does the heating/the shower work?

Como é que o aquecedor/o chuveiro trabalha?
koh-moo e kee oo akussuh-dor/oo shoovayroo trabal-yuh

Which day does the cleaner come?

Em que dia é que a mulher da limpeza vem?
ayng kuh dee-uh e kee uh mool-yehr duh leempay-zuh vayng

Is there any spare bedding?

Há alguma roupa de cama extra?
a algoomuh roh-puh duh kahmuh eshtruh

A fuse has blown

Rebentou um fusível
ruh-bentoh oom foozeevel

Where can I contact you?

Onde é que o posso contactar?
ondee e kee oo possoo kontaktar

Streetwise

Shops are generally open from 0900-1300 and 1500-1900 or 1930, Mon-Fri. Saturday opening is normally 0900-1700, but may vary according to region, time of year and type of shop. A shopping centre (centro comercial) does not close at lunch time and remains open until 2100 or even 2200 every day of the week including Sunday. Bargains are often to be found at markets – most towns have one every week.

Where is the main shopping area?	**Onde fica a zona comercial?** *onduh feekuh uh zonuh koomehr-see-al*
What time do the shops close?	**A que horas fecham as lojas?** *uh kee orush feshowng ush lojush*
How much does that cost?	**Quanta custa aquilo?** *kwantoo kooshtuh akeeloo*
How much is it per kilo/per metre?	**Quanto custa um quilo/um metro?** *kwantoo kooshtuh oom keeloo/oom metroo*
Can I try it on?	**Posso experimentar?** *possoo shpu-ree-mentar*
Where is the shoe/ food department?	**Onde fica a secção de sapataria/de comidas?** *onduh feekuh uh seksowng duh sapatuh-ree-uh/ duh koomeedush*
I'm looking for a gift for my wife	**Procuro uma prenda para a minha mulher** *prookooroo oomuh prenduh pra meen-yuh mool-yehr*
I'm just looking	**Estou só a ver** *shtoh so uh vehr*

See also **BUYING, PAYING**

SIGHTSEEING

What is there to see here?	**O que é que há para ver aqui?** *oo kee e kee a **pa**ruh vehr a**kee***
Excuse me, how do I get to the cathedral?	**Desculpe, como é que se vai para a catedral?** *dush**koolp koh**-moo e kuh suh vy pra katuh-**dral***
Where is the museum?	**Onde fica o museu?** *onduh **fee**kuh oo moo**za**yoo*
What time does the guided tour begin?	**A que horas é que a visita guiada começa?** *uh kee **or**uz e kee uh vee**zee**tuh ghee-ah-duh koo**mess**uh*
What time does the museum open?	**A que horas é que abre o museu?** *uh kee **or**uz e kee **ah**-bruh oo moo**za**yoo*
Is the castle open to the public?	**O castelo está aberto ao público?** *oo kash-**te**loo shta a**behr**-too ow **poo**blikoo*
How much does it cost to get in?	**Quanto custa o bilhete de entrada?** ***kwan**too **koosh**tuh oo beel-**yet** dayn-**trah**-duh*
Is there a reduction for children/senior citizens?	**Há um desconto para as crianças/os reformados?** *a oom dush-**kon**too prash kree-**an**sush/oosh ruh-foor**mah**-doosh*
Can we take photographs in here?	**Podemos tirar fotografias aqui?** *poo**day**-moosh tee**rar** footoogruh-**fee**-uz a**kee***

See also **MAPS & GUIDES, TRIPS & EXCURSIONS**

Streetwise

Most well-known brands of cigarette are readily available. The sign for no smoking is *Proibido fumar*. Smoking is forbidden in cinemas, in theatres and on buses.

Do you mind if I smoke?	**Importa-se se eu fumar?** *eemportuh-suh see ay-oo foomar*
May I have an ashtray?	**Pode-me dar um cinzeiro?** *pod-muh dar oom seenzay-roo*
Is this a no-smoking area?	**Esta zona é para não-fumadores?** *eshtuh zonuh e paruh nowng-foomuh-dorush*
A packet of ..., please	**Um maço de ... por favor** *oom mah-soo duh ... poor favor*
Have you got any American/English brands?	**Tem algumas marcas americanas/inglesas?** *tayng algoomush markuz ameree-kah-nush/eenglay-zush*
I'd like some pipe tobacco	**Quero tabaco para o cachimbo** *kehroo tabah-koo pro kasheemboo*
Do you have any matches/pipe cleaners?	**Tem fósforos/limpa-cachimbos?** *tayng fosh-fooroosh/leempuh-kasheemboosh*
Have you a gas refill for my lighter?	**Tem uma carga para este isqueiro?** *tayng oomuh karguh paruh aysht eeshkay-roo*
Have you got a light?	**Tem lume?** *tayng loom*

SPORTS

Which sports activities are available here?	**Que actividades desportivas se podem fazer aqui?** *kuh ateevee-**dah**-dush dushpoor-**tee**vush suh **pod**ayng fa**zehr** a**kee***
Is it possible to go fishing/riding?	**Pode-se ir pescar/andar a cavalo?** ***pod**-suh eer push**kar**/an**dar** uh ka**vah**-loo*
Where can we play tennis/golf?	**Onde podemos jogar ténis/golfe?** *onduh poo**day**-moosh joo**gar** **tay**-neesh/golf*
Is there a swimming pool?	**Há uma piscina?** *a **oom**uh peesh-**see**nuh*
Are there any interesting walks nearby?	**Vale a pena dar alguns passeios por aqui?** *val uh **pay**-nuh dar al**goonsh** pa-**say**oosh poor a**kee***
Can we rent the equipment?	**Podemos alugar o equipamento?** *poo**day**-mooz aloo**gar** oo eekeepuh-**men**too*
How much does it cost per hour?	**Quanto custa à hora?** ***kwan**too **koosh**tuh a **or**uh*
Do we need to be members?	**Temos que ser sócios?** ***tay**-moosh kuh sehr **soss**-yoosh*
Where do we buy our tickets?	**Onde compramos os bilhetes?** *onduh kom**prah**-mooz ooj beel-**yetsh***
Can we take lessons?	**Podemos ter lições?** *poo**day**-moosh tehr lee-**soynsh***

See also **BEACH, ENTERTAINMENT, WATERSPORTS**

Streetwise

You can either hail a taxi or pick one up at a stand. Taxis are green and black and the sign 'Alguer' means that the taxi is for hire. Make sure that the meter is on; if not, ask the price before setting off. A tip of around 10% is the norm. Expect surcharges at night and at weekends and for extra luggage.

Can you order me a taxi, please?	**Pode chamar-me um táxi?** *pod sha**mar**-muh oom **tax**ee*
To the main station/ airport, please	**Para a estação principal/o aeroporto, por favor** *pra shta**sowng** preensee**pal**/oo uh-ehroo-**por**too poor fa**vor***
Take me to this address	**Leve-me a esta morada** ***lev**-muh uh **esh**tuh moo**rah**-duh*
How much will it cost?	**Quanto custa?** *kwan too **koosh**tuh*
I'm in a hurry	**Tenho pressa** ***ten**-yoo **press**uh*
Can you wait here for a few minutes?	**Pode esperar aqui uns minutos?** *pod shpuh-**rar** a**kee** oonj mee**noo**toosh*
How much is it?	**Quanto é?** *kwan too e*
Keep the change	**Guarde o troco** *gward oo **tro**koo*
Make it … escudos	**Arredonde para …** (*see* NUMBERS) **escudos** *arruh-**dond** pa ruh … **shkoo**doosh*

TELEPHONE

Streetwise

Hotels often charge high rates for telephone calls so the cheapest way to phone is at a post office or from a phone box. You will find booths in the street or in bars – look for the blue sign 'telefone público'. For international calls it is easier to go to the post office exchange – you make a call in a booth and then pay for the number of units used. To call abroad, dial 00 before the country code. Phone cards (cartão de telefone) can be bought in post offices or shops.

I want to make a phone call	**Quero fazer uma chamada** *kehroo fazehr oomuh shamah-duh*
Can I have a line?	**Posso ligar?** *possoo leegar*
The number is …	**O número é …** (*see* NUMBERS) *oo noomeroo e …*
I want to reverse the charges	**Quero que seja pagável no destino** *kehroo kuh sejuh pagah-vel noo dushteenoo*
Have you got change for the phone?	**Tem dinheiro trocado para o telefone?** *tayng deen-yay-roo trookah-doo pro tuh-luh-fon*
What coins do I need?	**De que moedas preciso?** *duh kuh mway-dush pre-seezoo*
How much is it to phone Britain/the USA?	**Quanto custa telefonar para a Grã-Bretanha/para os Estados-Unidos?** *kwantoo kooshtuh tuh-luh-foonar pra grambruh-tahn-yuh/prosh shtah-doozoonee-doosh*
I can't get through	**Não consigo fazer a ligação** *nowng konseegoo fazehr uh leeguh-sowng*
The line's engaged	**Está impedido** *shta eempuh-deedoo*

TELEPHONE

Hello, this is … | **Allô, daqui fala …**
aloh dakee fah-luh

Can I speak to …? | **Posso falar com …?**
possoo falar kong …

I've been cut off | **Foi interrompida a ligação**
foy eenterom-peeduh uh leeguh-sowng

It's a bad line | **A ligação está má**
uh leeguh-sowng shta ma

YOU MAY HEAR:

Estou a tentar fazer a sua ligação
*shtoh uh tentar fazehr uh soo-uh
leeguh-sowng*

I'm trying to connect you

Consegui a ligação
konsuh-ghee uh leeguh-sowng

I'm putting you through

Não desligue
nowng duj-leeg

Hold the line

Lamento, está impedido
lamentoo shta eempuh-deedoo

I'm sorry, it's engaged

Por favor, volte a tentar mais tarde
poor favor volt uh tentar mysh tard

Please try again later

Quem fala?
kayng fah-luh

Who's calling?

Enganou-se no número
aynga-noh-suh noo noomeroo

Sorry, wrong number

TIME

vinte e uma horas	2100	9.00 pm
veentee oomuh orush		
dezasseis horas e quarenta e cinco minutos	1645	4.45 pm
dezuh-sayz oruz ee kwarentee seenkoo meenootoosh		

What's the time?	**Que horas são?**
	kee orush sowng
It's:	**São:**
	sowng
8.00	**oito horas**
	oytoo orush
8.05	**oito e cinco**
	oytoo ee seenkoo
8.10	**oito e dez**
	oytoo ee desh
8.15	**oito e um quarto**
	oytoo ee oom kwartoo
8.20	**oito e vinte**
	oytoo ee veent
8.25	**oito e vinte e cinco**
	oytoo ee veentee seenkoo
8.30	**oito e meia**
	oytoo ee mayuh
8.35	**nove menos vinte e cinco**
	nov may-noosh veentee seenkoo
8.40	**nove menos vinte**
	nov may-noosh veent
8.45	**nove menos um quarto**
	nov may-nooz oom kwartoo
8.50	**nove menos dez**
	nov may-noosh desh
8.55	**nove menos cinco**
	nov may-noosh seenkoo
12.00	**meio-dia** (midday); **meia-noite** (midnight)
	mayoo-dee-uh　　*mayuh-noyt*

See also **NUMBERS**

TIME PHRASES

What time do you open/close?
A que horas é que abre/fecha?
uh kee oruz e kee ah-bruh/feshuh

Do we have time to visit the town?
Temos tempo para visitar a cidade?
tay-moosh tempoo paruh veezeetar uh see-dahd

How long will it take to get there?
Quanto tempo demora a chegar lá?
kwantoo tempoo duh-moruh uh shuh-gar la

We can be there in half an hour
Chegamos lá em meia hora
shuh-gah-moosh la ayng mayuh oruh

We arrived early/late
Chegámos cedo/tarde
shuh-gamoosh say-doo/tard

We must be back at the hotel before … o'clock
Devemos regressar ao hotel antes das … (*see* TIME)
duh-vay-moosh ruh-gressar ow oh-tel antsh duz …

When does the coach leave in the morning?
A que horas parte o autocarro de manhã?
uh kee orush part oo owtoo-karroo duh man-yang

The tour starts at about half past three
A excursão começa por volta das três e meia
uh shkoor-sowng koomessuh poor voltuh dush trayz ee mayuh

The museum is open in the morning/afternoon
O museu está aberto de manhã/de tarde
oo moozay-oo shta abehr-too duh man-yang/duh tard

The table is booked for … o'clock this evening
A mesa está reservada para … (*see* TIME) **da noite**
uh may-zuh shta rezehr-vah-duh praz … duh noyt

TIPPING

Streetwise

You should tip usherettes, taxi drivers, porters, waiters, toilet attendants, staff in hairdresser's, etc. The tip should be between 50 and 100 escudos.

Sorry, I don't have any change	**Desculpe, mas não tenho troco** *dush**koolp** mush nowng **ten**-yoo **tro**koo*
Could you give me change of …?	**Podia trocar-me …?** *poo**dee**-uh troo**kar**-muh …*
Is it usual to tip …?	**É costume dar uma gorjeta …?** *e koosh-**toom** dar **oom**uh goor-**jet**uh …*
How much should I tip?	**Quanto é que devo dar?** ***kwan**too e kuh **dev**oo dar*
Is the tip included?	**A gorjeta está incluída?** *uh goor-**jet**uh shta een-**klwee**duh*
Keep the change	**Guarde o troco** *gward oo **tro**koo*
Make it … escudos	**Arredonde para …** (*see* NUMBERS) **escudos** *arruh-**dond** p**a**ruh … **shkoo**doosh*

See also EATING OUT, TAXIS

Streetwise

In Portugal you will have to pay to use public toilets. However, it's customary to use the toilets in cafés and bars, though you should tip the attendant if there is one. 'Superloos' are being installed at strategic places in cities – look for the familiar oval box with the sign 'sanitário' on top.

Where is the Gents'/ the Ladies'?	**Onde está a casa de banho dos homens/ das senhoras?** *onduh shta uh kah-zuh duh bahn-yoo dooz omaynsh/dush sun-yorush*
Do you have to pay?	**Tem que se pagar?** *tayng kuh suh pagar*
This toilet does not flush	**O autoclismo não trabalha** *oo owto-kleej-moo nowng trabal-yuh*
There is no toilet paper/soap	**Não há papel higiénico/sabonete** *nowng a papel eej-yenikoo/saboonet*
Do I have to pay extra to use the washbasin?	**Tenho que pagar extra para usar o lavatório?** *ten-yoo kuh pagar eshtruh paruh oozar oo lavuh-tor-yoo*
Is there a toilet for the disabled?	**Há casa de banho para deficientes?** *a kah-zuh duh bahn-yoo paruh duh-feess-yentsh*
Are there facilities for mothers with babies?	**Há instalações para mães com bebés?** *a een-shtalluh-soynsh paruh mynsh kong bebesh*
The towels have run out	**Já não há toalhas** *jah nowng a too-al-yush*
The door will not close	**A porta não se fecha** *uh portuh nowng suh feshuh*

TRAIN TRAVEL

Streetwise

Is this the train for …?

É este o comboio para …?
*e aysht oo kom**boy**oo **pa**ruh …*

Is this seat free?

Este lugar está vago?
*aysht loo**gar** shta **vah**-goo*

I have a seat
reservation

Eu tenho um lugar marcado
*ay-oo **ten**-yoo oom loo**gar** mar**kah**-doo*

Can you help me
put my suitcase on
the luggage rack?

Pode ajudar-me a pôr a mala na rede?
*pod ajoo**dar**-muh uh por uh **mah**-luh nuh red*

May I open the
window?

Posso abrir a janela?
***poss**oo a**breer** uh ja**nel**uh*

What time do we
get to …?

A que horas chegamos a …?
*uh kee **or**ush shuh-**gah**-mooz uh …*

Do we stop at …?

Paramos em …?
*pa**rah**-mooz ayng …*

Where do I change
for …?

Onde é que mudo para …?
***on**dee e kuh **moo**doo **pa**ruh …*

Is there a restaurant
car?

Há um vagão restaurante?
*a oom va**gowng** rushtoh-**rant***

See also **LUGGAGE, RAILWAY STATION**

TRAVEL AGENT

What's the best way to get to …?	**Qual é o melhor caminho para …?** *kwal e oo mel-yor kameen-yoo paruh …*
How much is it to fly to …?	**Quanto custa um voo para …?** *kwantoo kooshtuh oom voh-oo paruh …*
Are there any special cheap fares?	**Há alguns bilhetes especiais mais baratos?** *a algoonsh beel-yetsh shpussee-ysh mysh barah-toosh*
What times are the trains/flights?	**A que horas são os comboios/os voos?** *uh kee orush sowng oosh komboyoosh/oosh voh-oosh*
Can I buy the tickets here?	**Posso comprar os bilhetes aqui?** *possoo komprar ooj beel-yetz akee*
Can I change my booking?	**Posso alterar a minha marcação?** *possoo alterar uh meen-yuh markuh-sowng*
Can you book me on the London flight?	**Pode marcar-me passagem para o voo de Londres?** *pod markar-muh pasah-jayng pro voh-oo duh londrush*
Can I get back to Manchester tonight?	**Posso regressar a Manchester esta noite?** *possoo ruh-gruh-sar uh Manchester eshtuh noyt*
Two second-class returns to …	**Dois bilhetes de ida e volta em segunda classe para …** *doysh beel-yetsh deeduh ee voltuh ayng segoonduh klass paruh …*
Can you book me into a hotel?	**Pode reservar-me um hotel?** *pod ruh-zer-var-muh oom oh-tel*

TRIPS & EXCURSIONS

Are there any
sightseeing tours?

Há excursões guiadas?
a shkoor-soynsh ghee-ah-dush

When is the bus tour
of the town?

Quando é a visita guiada à cidade?
*kwandoo e uh veezeetuh ghee-ah-duh a
seedahd*

How long does the
tour take?

Quanto tempo demora a visita?
kwantoo tempoo duh-moruh uh veezeetuh

Are there any boat
trips on the river/
lake?

Há passeios de barco no rio/lago?
a pasayoosh duh barkoo noo ree-oo/lah-goo

Are there any
guided tours of
the cathedral?

Há algumas visitas guiadas à catedral?
*a algoomush veezeetush ghee-ah-duz a
katuh-dral*

Is there a reduction
for a group?

Há desconto para grupos?
a dush-kontoo paruh groopoosh

Is there a reduction
for senior citizens?

Há desconto para reformados?
a dush-kontoo paruh refoormah-doosh

Where do we stop
for lunch?

Onde paramos para almoçar?
onduh parah-moosh paruh almoosar

Please stop the bus,
my child is feeling
sick!

**Por favor, pare o autocarro, o meu filho
está enjoado**
*poor favor pahr oo owtoo-karroo oo mayoo
feel-yoo shta aynj-wah-doo*

See also **SIGHTSEEING**

Is it possible to go water-skiing/ windsurfing?	**É possível fazer ski/wind-surf?** *e poo-**see**vel fa**zehr** shkee/windsurf*
Can we rent a motorboat?	**Podemos alugar um barco a motor?** *poo**day**-mooz aloo**gar** oom **bar**koo uh moo**tor***
Can I rent a sailboard?	**Posso alugar uma prancha?** *poss**oo aloo**gar** oom**uh **pran**shuh*
Can one swim in the river?	**Pode-se nadar no rio?** ***pod**-suh na**dar** noo **ree**-oo*
Can we fish here?	**Podemos pescar aqui?** *poo**day**-moosh push**kar** a**kee***
Is there a paddling pool for the children?	**Há uma piscina para crianças?** *a **oom**uh peesh-**see**nuh **pa**ruh kree-**an**sush*
Do you give lessons?	**Dá lições?** *da lee-**soynsh***
Where is the public swimming pool?	**Onde é a piscina municipal?** ***on**dee e uh peesh-**see**nuh mooneesee-**pal***
Is the pool heated?	**A piscina é aquecida?** *uh peesh-**see**nuh e akuh-**see**duh*
Is it an outdoor pool?	**A piscina é descoberta?** *uh peesh-**see**nuh e dushkoo-**behr**-tuh*

See also **BEACH**

WEATHER

It's a lovely day

Está um dia lindo
*shta oom **dee**-uh **leen**doo*

What dreadful
weather!

Que tempo horrível!
*kuh **tem**poo oh-**ree**vel*

It is raining/snowing

Está a chover/nevar
*shta uh shoo**vehr**/nuh-**var***

It's windy/foggy

Está vento/nevoeiro
*shta **ven**too/nuv-**way**roo*

There's a nice
breeze blowing

Sopra um ventinho agradável
***sop**ruh oom ven**teen**-yoo agruh-**dah**-vel*

Will it be cold
tonight?

Vai estar frio esta noite?
*vy shtar **free**-oo **esh**tuh noyt*

Is it going to rain/
to snow?

Vai chover/nevar?
*vy shoo**vehr**/nuh-**var***

Will there be a
frost?

Vai cair geada?
*vy kuh-**eer** jee-**ah**-duh*

Will there be a
thunderstorm?

Vai fazer trovoada?
*vy fa**zehr** troov-**wah**-duh*

Is it going to be
fine?

Vai estar bom tempo?
*vy shtar bong **tem**poo*

Is the weather going
to change?

O tempo vai mudar?
*oo **tem**poo vy moo**dar***

What is the
temperature?

Qual é a temperatura?
*kwal e uh temperuh-**too**ruh*

Wines in Portugal are extremely good value wherever you go and even house wines can be of a surprisingly high quality. Particularly good are the red table wines and *vinho verde*, 'green wine', a young, usually semi-sparkling, white or red wine made principally in the north west of Portugal. Among the main wine-producing regions are:

> Bucelas (dry gold-coloured wines),
> Colares (light and sharp reds),
> Dão (fruity reds and whites), and of course
> Douro (Ports) and
> Madeira (dessert or aperitif wines).

Like many other wine-producing nations, Portugal operates a quality control system. Look for the words *Denominacão de Origen (DO)* on the label of a bottle – this denotes that the wine comes from one of the ten demarcated areas *(região demarcada)* where only high-quality grapes are used and the production process is strictly controlled.

Portugal is of course closely associated with port *(vinho do Porto)* which takes its name not from the country but from the town of Oporto. If you are in that area it's well worth visiting one of the wine lodges to sample some of the local produce. Port is a sweet, fortified wine made from a variety of grapes blended with a little brandy. Most ports have to be allowed to mature for a number of years before they will be ready to be enjoyed at their best. Port is however drunk less in Portugal than abroad.

Most well-known brands of spirits are available in Portugal. Particular to the country are its own brandy-type drinks, *aguardente velhas*, and a strong, clear spirit made from grapes called *bagaço*. Also popular are various liqueurs such as *ginja* (cherry liqueur) and *amêndoa amarga* (sweet almond liqueur).

The following terms may be helpful:

tinto/branco	red/white
vinho da casa/de mesa	house/table wine
espumante/espumoso	sparkling
rosé/rosado	rosé
doce/seco	sweet/dry
encorpado	full-bodied

We'd like an aperitif	**Queríamos um aperitivo** *kree-uh-mooz oom aperuh-teevoo*
May I have the wine list, please?	**Pode-me dar a lista de vinhos, por favor?** *pod-muh dar uh leeshtuh duh veen-yoosh poor favoor*
Can you recommend a good red/white/ rosé wine?	**Pode recomendar-nos um bom vinho tinto/branco/rosé?** *pod ruh-koomendar-nooz oom bong veen-yoo teentoo/brankoo/roh-zay*
A bottle/carafe of house wine	**Uma garrafa/um jarro de vinho da casa** *oomuh garrah-fuh/oom jarroo duh veen-yoo duh kah-zuh*
A half bottle of …	**Meia garrafa de …** *mayuh garrah-fuh duh …*
Would you bring another glass, please?	**Pode trazer um outro copo, por favor?** *pod trazehr oom oh-troo kopoo poor favor*
This wine is not chilled	**O vinho não está fresco** *oo veen-yoo nowng shta freshkoo*
What liqueurs do you have?	**Que licores tem?** *kuh lee-korush tayng*
I'll have a brandy/a Scotch	**Quero um brandy/um whisky** *kehroo oom brandee/oom weeshkee*
A gin and tonic	**Um gin tónico** *oom jin tonikoo*
A Martini and lemonade	**Um martini com limonada** *oom marteenee kong leemoo-nah-duh*

See also **DRINKS, EATING OUT, ORDERING**

a um (uma) *oom (oomuh)*

abbey a abadia *abuh-dee-uh*

about cerca de *sehr-kuh duh*; **about ten o'clock** por volta das dez *poor voltuh dush desh*

above por cima de *poor seemuh duh*

accident o acidente *aseedent*

accommodation o alojamento *alojuh-mentoo*

ache a dor *dor*; **my head aches** doi-me a cabeça *doy-muh uh kabay-shuh*

adaptor *(electrical)* o adaptador *adaptuh-dor*

address a morada *moorah-duh*

adhesive tape a fita adesiva *feetuh aduh-zeevuh*

admission charge o bilhete de entrada *beel-yet dayn-trah-duh*

adult o/a adulto(a) *adooltoo(uh)*

advance: in advance antecipadamente *antussuh-pah-duh-ment*

African africano(a) *afree-kah-noo(uh)*

after depois *duh-poysh*

afternoon a tarde *tard*

aftershave o aftershave *aftershave*

again outra vez *oh-truh vesh*

agent o agente *ajent*

ago: a week ago há uma semana *a oomuh semah-nuh*

air conditioning o ar condicionado *ar kondeess-yoonah-doo*

airline a linha aérea *leen-yuh auh-ehr-yuh*

air mail a via aérea *vee-uh uh-ehr-yuh*

air mattress o colchão pneumático *kol-showng pnay-oomatikoo*

airport o aeroporto *uh-ehroo-portoo*

aisle a coxia *coo-shee-uh*

alarm o alarme *uhlarm*

alcohol o álcool *alk-wol*

alcoholic alcoólico(a) *alk-wolikoo(uh)*

all todo(a), todos(as) *toh-doo(uh), toh-doosh(ush)*

allergic alérgico(a) *alehr-jikoo(uh)*

all right *(agreed)* está bem *shta bayng*; **are you all right?** você está bem? *voh-se shta bayng*

almost quase *kwahz*

also também *tambayng*

always sempre *sempruh*

am *see* GRAMMAR

ambulance a ambulância *amboo-lanss-yuh*

America a América *amerikuh*

American americano(a) *amuh-ree-kah-noo(uh)*

anaesthetic o anestésico *anush-tezikoo*

and e *ee*

anorak a anorak *anoorak*

another um(a) outro(a) *oom(uh) oh-troo(uh)*; **another beer?** mais uma cerveja? *myz oomuh servay-juh*

antibiotic o antibiótico *anteebee-otikoo*

antifreeze o anticongelante *anteekon-jelant*

antiseptic o antiséptico *antee-septikoo*

any: have you any apples? tem algumas maçãs? *tayng algoomush masansh*

apartment o apartamento *apartuh-mentoo*
aperitif o aperitivo *apuh-ree-teevoo*
apple a maçã *masang*
appointment o encontro *ayng-kontroo*
apricot o damasco *damashkoo*
are see GRAMMAR
arm o braço *brah-soo*
armbands (for swimming) as braçadeiras *brassuh-day-rush*
arrival a chegada *shuh-gah-duh*
arrive chegar *shuh-gar*
art gallery o museo de arte *moozay-oo dart*
artichoke a alcachofra *alkuh-shofruh*
ashtray o cinzeiro *seenzay-roo*
asparagus o espargo *shpargoo*
aspirin a aspirina *ashpee-reenuh*
asthma a asma *ajmuh*
at em *ayng*; **at home** em casa *ayng kahzuh*
aubergine a beringela *bereen-jeluh*
Australia a Austrália *owsh-trah-lee-uh*
Australian australiano(a) *owsh-tralee-ah-noo(uh)*
automatic automático(a) *owtoo-matikoo(uh)*
autumn o outono *oh-toh-noo*
avocado o abacate *abakat*

baby o bebé *bebe*
baby food a comida de bebé *koomeeduh duh bebe*
baby-sitter a babysitter *babysitter*

back (of body) as costas *koshtush*
backpack a mochila *moosheeluh*
bacon o toucinho *toh-seen-yoo*
bad (food) estragado(a) *shtra-gah-doo(uh)*; (weather, news) mau (má) *mow (ma)*
bag o saco *sah-koo*; (suitcase) a mala *mah-luh*
baggage a bagagem *bagah-jayung*
baggage reclaim o tapete rolante *tapet roolant*
baker's a padaria *paduh-ree-uh*
balcony o balcão *balkowng*
ball a bola *boluh*
banana a banana *banah-nuh*
band (musical) a banda musical *banduh moozee-kal*
bandage a ligadura *leeguh-dooruh*
bank o banco *bankoo*
bar o bar *bar*
barber o barbeiro *barbay-roo*
basket o cesto *seshtoo*
bath o banho *bahn-yoo*; **to take a bath** tomar banho *toomar bahn-yoo*
bathing cap a touca de banho *toh-kuh duh bahn-yoo*
bathroom a casa de banho *kah-zuh duh bahn-yoo*
battery (for car) a bateria *batuh-ree-uh*
be see GRAMMAR
beach a praia *pry-uh*
bean o feijão *fay-jowng*
beautiful belo(a) *beloo(uh)*
bed a cama *kah-muh*
bedding a roupa de cama *roh-puh duh kah-muh*

bedroom o quarto *kwartoo*

beef a carne de vaca *karn duh vah-kuh*

beer a cerveja *servay-juh*

beetroot a beterraba *betuh-rah-buh*

before antes de *antsh duh*

begin começar *koomuh-sar*

behind atrás *atrash*

below por baixo de *poor byshoo duh*

belt o cinto *seentoo*

beside ao lado de *ow lah-doo duh*

best o/a melhor *mul-yor*

better (than) melhor (do que) *mul-yor (doo kuh)*

between entre *entruh*

bicycle a bicicleta *beesee-kletuh*

big grande *grand*

bigger maior *mayor*

bikini o biquini *beekeenee*

bill a conta *kontuh*

bin o caixote do lixo *ky-shot doo leeshoo*

binoculars os binóculos *bee-nokooloosh*

bird o pássaro *passuh-roo*

birthday o aniversário *aneever-sar-yoo*

birthday card o cartão de aniversário *kartowng daneever-sar-yoo*

bit: a bit of um bocado (de) *oom bookah-doo (duh)*

bitten mordido(a) *mordee-doo(uh)*; (by insect) picado(a) *peekah-doo(uh)*

bitter amargo(a) *amargoo(uh)*

black preto(a) *pray-too(uh)*

blackcurrant a groselha *groozel-yuh*

blanket o cobertor *koobertor*

bleach a lixívia *leesheev-yuh*

blocked bloqueado(a) *blook-yah-doo(uh)*

blood group o grupo sanguíneo *groopoo sangeen-yoo*

blouse a blusa *bloozuh*

blow-dry o brushing *brushing*

blue azul *azool*

boarding card o cartão de embarque *kartowng daym-bark*

boarding house a pensão *payn-sowng*

boat o barco *barkoo*

boat trip a viagem de barco *vee-ah-jayng duh barkoo*

boiled cozido(a) *coozeedoo(uh)*

book[1] *n* o livro *leevroo*; **book of tickets** a caderneta de bilhetes *kader-netuh duh beel-yetsh*

book[2] *vb* reservar *rezervar*

booking a marcação *markuh-sowng*

booking office a bilheteira *beel-yuh-tay-ruh*

bookshop a livraria *leevruh-ree-uh*

boots as botas *botush*

border a fronteira *frontay-ruh*

both ambos(as) *amboosh(ush)*

bottle a garrafa *garrah-fuh*

bottle-opener o abre-garrafas *abruh-garrah-fush*

box a caixa *ky-shuh*

box office a bilheteira *beel-yuh-tay-ruh*

boy o rapaz *rapash*

boyfriend o namorado *namoo-rah-doo*

bra o soutien *soot-yang*

bracelet a pulseira *poolsay-ruh*

brake fluid o óleo dos travões *ol-yoo doosh tra voynsh*

brakes os travões *travoynsh*

brandy a aguardente *agwar-dent*

bread o pão *powng*

breakable frágil *frah-jeel*

breakdown a avaria *avuh-ree-uh*

breakdown van o pronto-socorro *pront-sookorroh*

breakfast o pequeno almoço *puh-kay-noo almoh-soo*

breast *(chicken)* o peito *paytoo*

briefcase a pasta *pashtuh*

bring trazer *trazehr*

Britain a Grã-Bretanha *grambruh-tahn-yuh*

British britânico(a) *bree-tahnikoo(uh)*

brochure a brochura *broshooruh*

broken partido(a) *perteedoo(uh)*

broken down *(machine, car)* avariado(a) *avuh-ree-ahdoo(uh)*

brooch o broche *brosh*

broom a vassoura *vasoh-ruh*

brother o irmão *eermowng*

brown castanho(a) *kashtahn-yoo(uh)*

brush a escova *shkovuh*

Brussels sprouts as couves de Bruxelas *kohvsh duh broo-selush*

bucket o balde *balduh*

buffet o bufete *boofet*

buffet car o vagão restaurante *vagowng rushtoh-rant*

bulb a lâmpada *lahm-paduh*

bureau de change a casa de câmbio *kah-zuh duh kamb-yoo*

burst rebentado(a) *ruh-ben-tahdoo(uh)*

bus o autocarro *owtoo-karroo*

business os negócios *negoss-yoosh*

bus station a estação de autocarros *shtasowng dowtoo karroosh*

bus stop a paragem de autocarro *parah-jayng dowtoo-karroo*

bus tour a excursão de autocarro *shkoor-sowng dowtoo-karroo*

busy ocupado(a) *oh-koopah-doo(uh)*

but mas *mush*

butcher's o talho *tal-yoo*

butter a manteiga *mantay-guh*

button o botão *bootowng*

buy comprar *komprar*

by *(close to)* perto de *pehrtoo duh; (via)* por *poor; (beside)* ao lado de *ow lah-doo duh*

bypass o desvio *duj-vee-oo*

cabaret o espectáculo de variedades *shpe-takooloo duh varee-uh-dahdush*

cabbage a couve *kohv*

cable car o teleférico *tuh-luh-ferikoo*

café o café *kuh-fe*

cagoule o kispo *keeshpoo*

cake o bolo *boh-loo*

call[1] *vb* chamar *shamar*

call[2] *n (on telephone)* uma chamada *shamah-duh;* **a long-distance call** uma chamada interurbana *shamah-duh eenter-oorbahna*

calm calmo(a) *kalmoo(uh)*
camera a máquina fotográfica *makinuh footoo-grafikuh*
camp acampar *akampar*
camp site o parque de campismo *park duh kampeej-moo*
can[1] *n* a lata *lah-tuh*
can[2] *vb (to be able)* poder *podehr*
Canada o Canadá *kanuh-da*
Canadian canadiano(a) *kanadee-ah-noo(uh)*
cancel cancelar *kansuh-lar*
canoe a canoa *kanoh-uh*
can-opener o abre-latas *abruh-lah-tush*
car o carro *karroo*
carafe o jarro *jarroo*
caravan a caravana *karuh-vah-nuh*
carburettor o carburador *karbooruh-dor*
card *(greetings)* o cartão *kartowng*; *(playing)* a carta *kartuh*
cardigan o casaco de lã *kazah-koo duh lang*
careful cuidadoso(a) *kweeduh-doh-zoo(uh)*
car park o parque de estacionamento *park duh shtass-yoonuh-mentoo*
carpet o tapete *tapet*
carriage *(railway)* a carruagem *kar-wah-jayng*
carrot a cenoura *suh-noh-ruh*
carry transportar *transh-poortar*
car wash a lavagem automática *lavah-jayng owtoo-matikuh*
case *(suitcase)* a mala *mah-luh*
cash[1] *vb (cheque)* levantar *luh-vantar*

cash[2] *n* o dinheiro *deen-yay-roo*
cash desk a caixa *ky-shuh*
cashier o caixa *ky-shuh*
casino o casino *kazeenoo*
cassette a cassette *kaset*
castle o castelo *kashteloo*
catch apanhar *apan-yar*
cathedral a catedral *katuh-dral*
Catholic católico(a) *ka-tolikoo(uh)*
cauliflower a couve-flor *kohv-flor*
cave a caverna *kavehr-nuh*
celery o aipo *y-poo*
cemetery o cemitério *suh-mee-tehr-yoo*
centimetre o centímetro *sen-teemetroo*
central central *sentral*
centre o centro *sentroo*
cereal *(for breakfast)* o cereal *suh-ree-al*
certain *(sure)* certo(a) *sehrtoo(uh)*
certificate o certificado *serteefee-kah-doo*
chain a corrente *koorent*
chair a cadeira *kaday-ruh*
chalet a vivenda *veevenduh*
champagne o champanhe *shampan-yuh*
change[1] *n (money)* o troco *troh-koo*
change[2] *vb (money)* trocar *trookar*; *(clothes)* mudar *moodar*
changing room o gabinete de provas *gabeenet duh provush*
chapel a capela *kapeluh*
charge o custo *kooshtoo*
cheap barato(a) *barah-too(uh)*

cheaper mais barato(a) *mysh barah-too(uh)*

check verificar *veree-feekar*

check in fazer o check-in *fazehr oo check-in*

check-in desk o balcão do check-in *balkowng doo check-in*

cheerio adeus *aday-oosh*

cheers saúde! *sa-ood*

cheese o queijo *kay-joo*

chemist's a farmácia *farmass-yuh*

cheque o cheque *shek*

cheque book o livro de cheques *leevroo duh sheksh*

cheque card o cartão garantia *kartowng garan-tee-uh*

cherry a cereja *suh-ray-juh*

chestnut a castanha *kashtahn-yuh*

chewing gum a pastilha elástica *pashteel-yuh eelash-tikuh*

chicken a galinha *galeen-yuh*

chickenpox a varicela *varee-seluh*

child a criança *kree-ansuh*

children as crianças *kree-ansush*

chilli a malagueta *maluh-getuh*

chips as batatas fritas *batah-tush freetush*

chocolate o chocolate *shookoo-lat*

chocolates as chocolates *shookoolatsh*

Christmas o Natal *natal*

church a igreja *ee-grejuh*

cider a sidra *seedruh*

cigar o charuto *sharootoo*

cigarette o cigarro *seegarroo*

cigarette papers as mortalhas *moortalyush*

cinema o cinema *seenay-muh*

circus o circo *seerkoo*

city a cidade *seedahd*

clean[1] *adj* limpo(a) *leempoo(uh)*

clean[2] *vb* limpar *leempar*

cleansing cream o creme de limpeza *krem duh leempay-zuh*

client o/a cliente *klee-ent*

climbing o alpinismo *alpee-neejmoo*

climbing boots as botas de alpinismo *botush dalpee-neejmoo*

cloakroom o vestiário *vushtee-ar-yoo*

clock o relógio *reloj-yoo*

close[1] *adj* (near) perto *pehrtoo*

close[2] *vb* fechar *feshar*

closed fechado(a) *fushah-doo(uh)*

cloth o tecido *tuh-seedoo*

clothes as roupas *roh-push*

clothes peg a mola da roupa *moluh duh roh-puh*

cloudy nublado(a) *nooblah-doo(uh)*

clove o cravinho *kraveen-yoo*

club o clube *kloob*

coach (bus) o autocarro *owtoo-karroo*; (train) a carruagem *karwah-jayng*

coach trip a viagem de autocarro *vee-ah-jayng dowtoo-karroo*

coast a costa *koshtuh*

coastguard o guarda fiscal *gwarduh feeshkal*

coat o casaco *kazah-koo*

coat hanger o cabide *kabeed*

cocktail o cocktail *cocktail*

cocoa o cacau *kakow*

coconut o coco *koh-koo*

coffee o café *kuh-fe*; **white coffee** o café com leite *kuh-fe kong layt*; **black coffee** o café *kuh-fe*

coin a moeda *mway-duh*

Coke ® a coca cola *kokuh-koluh*

colander o coador *koh-uh-dor*

cold[1] *n* o frio *free-oo*

cold[2] *adj* frio(a) *free-oo(uh)*; **I'm cold** tenho frio *ten-yoo free-oo*

colour a cor *kor*

comb o pente *pent*

come vir *veer*; *(arrive)* chegar *shuh-gar*; **to come back** voltar *voltar*; **to come in** entrar *ayn-trar*; **come in!** entre! *entruh*

comfortable confortável *komfoor-tah-vel*

communion o comunhão *koomoon-yowng*

company a companhia *kompan-yee-uh*

compartment o compartimento *compartee-mentoo*

complain queixar-se (de) *kay-shar-suh (duh)*

compulsory obrigatório(a) *oh-breeguh-tor-yoo(uh)*

computer o computador *kompootuh-dor*

concert o concerto *konsehr-too*

condensed milk o leite condensado *layt konden-sah-doo*

conditioner o acondicionador *akondeess-yoonuh-dor*

conductor *(on bus)* o cobrador *koobruh-dor*

conference a conferência *komfuh-renss-yuh*

confession a confissão *komfee-sowng*

confirm confirmar *komfeermar*

congratulations! parabéns! *paruh-baynsh*

connection a ligação *leeguh-sowng*

constipated com prisão de ventre *kong preezowng duh ventruh*

consulate o consulado *konsoolah-doo*

contact o contacto *kontaktoo*

contact lens cleaner o líquido para as lentes de contacto *leekidoo prash lentsh duh kontaktoo*

contact lenses as lentes de contacto *lentsh duh kontaktoo*

Continental breakfast o pequeno almoço continental *puh-kay-noo almoh-soo kontee-nental*

contraceptive o anticonceptivo *antee-konsep-teevoo*

cook cozinhar *koozenyar*

cooker o fogão *foogowng*

cool fresco(a) *freshkoo(uh)*

copy[1] *n* a cópia *kop-yuh*

copy[2] *vb* copiar *koop-yar*

corkscrew o saca-rolhas *sakuh-rol-yush*

corner o canto *kantoo*

cortisone a cortisona *koortee-zonuh*

cosmetics os cosméticos *kooj-metikoosh*

cost custar *kooshtar*; **how much does it/do they cost?** quanto custa/custam? *kwantoo kooshtuh/kooshtowng*

cotton o algodão *algoodowng*

cotton wool o algodão em rama *algoodowng* ayng **rah**-muh

couchette a couchette *koo***shet**

cough a tosse *tohss*

country *(not town)* o campo **kam***poo*; *(nation)* o país pa-**eesh**

couple *(two people)* o casal *ka***zal**

courgette a courgette *koor***jet**

courier o guia turístico *ghee*-uh too-**reesh***tikoo*

course *(of meal)* o prato **prah**-too

cover charge o serviço *ser***vee***soo*

crab o caranguejo *karan*-**gejoo**

crash o choque *shok*

crash helmet o capacete *kapuh*-**set**

cream *(lotion)* o creme *krem*; *(on milk)* a nata **nah**-tuh

credit card o cartão de crédito *kar***towng** deh **kred***itoo*

crisps as batatas fritas *batah*-tush **free**-tush

croquette o croquete *kro***ket**

cross *(road)* cruzar *kroo***zar**

crossed line as linhas cruzadas *leen*-yush kroo**zah**-dush

crossroads a encruzilhada *ayn-kroozeel*-**yah**-duh

crowded cheio(a) de gente *shay*oo(uh) duh jent

cruise o cruzeiro *kroo***zay**-roo

cucumber o pepino *puh*-**pee***noo*

cup a chávena *sha***venuh**

cupboard o aparador *aparuh*-**dor**

currant a groselha *groo***zel**-yuh

current a corrente *koo***rent**

cushion a almofada *almoo***fah**-duh

custard a nata **nah**-tuh

customs a alfândega *al*-**fanduh**-guh

cut[1] *n* o corte *kort*

cut[2] *vb* cortar *koor***tar**; **we've been cut off** foi interrompida a ligação *foy eenteram*-**pee***duh uh leeguh*-**sowng**

cutlery os talheres *tal*-**yeh***rush*

cycle a bicicleta *beesee*-**kle***tuh*

cycling o ciclismo *see***kleej***moo*

daily *(each day)* cada dia **kah**-duh **dee**-uh

damage *n* o prejuízo *pruh*-**jwee**-zoo

damp húmido(a) *oom***idoo(uh)**

dance[1] *n* o baile *byle*

dance[2] *vb* dançar *dan***sar**

dangerous perigoso(a) *peree*-**goh***zoo(uh)*

dark escuro(a) *shkoo***roo(uh)**

date a data **dah**-tuh

date of birth a data de nascimento **dah**-tuh duh nash-**see***mentoo*

daughter a filha **feel**-yuh

day o dia **dee**-uh

dear caro(a) **kah**-roo(uh)

decaffeinated coffee o café descafeinado *kuh*-**fe** dush-*kafay*-**nah**-doo

deck chair a cadeira de lona *ka***day**-ruh duh **lon***uh*

declare declarar *duh*-kla**rar**

deep fundo(a) **foon***doo(uh)*

defrost descongelar *dush*-konjuh-**lar**

de-ice descongelar *dush*-konjuh-**lar**

delay a demora *duh*-**mo***ruh*

delicious delicioso(a) *duh*-leess-**yoh**-zoo(uh)

dentist o/a dentista *denteeshtuh*

dentures a dentadura postiça
dentuh-dooruh poosh-teesuh

deodorant o desodorizante *duz-oh-dooree-zant*

department store o grande
armazém *grand armuh-zayng*

departure lounge a sala de espera
para partidas *sah-luh dushpehruh
paruh perteedush*

departures as partidas *perteedush*

deposit o depósito *duh-pozitoo*

dessert a sobremesa *sobruh-mayzuh*

details os pormenores *poormuh-
norush*

detergent o detergente *duh-terjent*

detour o desvio *duj-vee-oo*

develop desenvolver *duz-aym-
volvehr*

diabetic diabético(a) *dee-uh-
betikoo(uh)*

dialling code o indicativo
eendeekuh-teevoo

diamond o diamante *dee-uh-mant*

diarrhoea a diarreia *dee-uh-rayuh*

diary o diário *dee-ar-yoo*

dictionary o dicionário *deess-
yoonar-yoo*

diesel o gasóleo *gazol-yoo*

diet a dieta *dee-etuh*

different diferente *deefuh-rent*

difficult difícil *deefeeseel*

dinghy o bote *bot*

dining room a sala de jantar *sah-
luh duh jantar*

dinner o jantar *jantar*

direct *(train etc)* directo(a)
deeretoo(uh)

directory a lista telefónica *leeshtuh
tuh-luh-fonikuh*

dirty sujo(a) *soojoo(uh)*

disabled deficiente *duh-feess-yent*

disco a discoteca *deeshkoo-tekuh*

discount o desconto *dushkontoo*

dish o prato *prah-too*

dishwasher a máquina de lavar
louça *makinuh duh lavar loh-suh*

disinfectant o desinfectante
duzeem-fektant

distilled water a água destilada
ahg-wuh dushtee-lah-duh

divorced divorciado(a) *deevoorsee-
ah-doo(uh)*

dizzy tonto(a) *tontoo(uh)*

do fazer *fazehr*

doctor o doutor *doh-tor*

documents os documentos *dookoo-
mentoosh*

doll a boneca *boonekuh*

dollar o dólar *dolar*

door a porta *portuh*

double o dobro *doh-broo*

double bed a cama de casal *kah-
muh duh kazal*

double room o quarto de casal
kwartoo kuh kazal

doughnut a bola de Berlim *boluh
duh berleeng*

down para baixo *paruh by-shoo*; **to
go down** descer *dush-sehr*

downstairs lá em baixo *la ayng by-
shoo*

draught a corrente de ar *koorent
dar*

dress[1] *n* o vestido *vushteedoo*

dress[2] *vb* : **to get dressed** vestir-se *vushteer-suh*

dressing *(for food)* o tempero *tempay-roo*

drink[1] *n* a bebida *buh-beeduh*

drink[2] *vb* beber *buh-behr*

drinking chocolate o chocolate *shookoo-lat*

drinking water a água potável *ahg-wuh pootah-vel*

drive conduzir *kondoozeer*

driver *(of car)* o condutor *kondootor*

driving licence a carta de condução *kartuh duh kondoo-sowng*

drunk bêbedo(a) *bay-buh-doo(uh)*

dry[1] *adj* seco(a) *say-koo(uh)*

dry[2] *vb* secar *suh-kar*

dry-cleaner's a limpeza a seco *leempay-zuh uh say-koo*

duck o pato *pah-too*

dummy a chupeta *shoopetuh*

during durante *doorant*

duty-free isento de direitos *eezentoo duh deeray-toosh*

duty-free shop a loja franca *lojuh frankuh*

duvet o edredão *edruh-downg*

dynamo o dínamo *deenamoo*

each cada *kah-duh*

ear a orelha *oh-rel-yuh*

earache as dores do ouvidos *dorush doh-veedoosh*

earlier mais cedo *mysh say-doo*

early cedo *say-doo*

earrings os brincos *breenkoosh*

east o leste *lesht*

Easter a Páscoa *pashk-wuh*

easy fácil *fah-seel*

eat comer *koomehr*

egg o ovo *oh-voo*; **eggs** os ovos *oh-voosh*; **fried egg** ovo estrelado *oh-voo shtrelahdoo*; **hard-boiled egg** ovo cozido *oh-voo coozeedoo*; **scrambled eggs** os ovos mexidos *oh-voos meshidoosh*

either: either one um ou outro *oom oh oh-troo*

elastic elástico(a) *eelash-tikoo(uh)*

elastic band o elástico *eelash-tikoo*

electric eléctrico(a) *eeletrikoo(uh)*

electrician o electricista *eletree-seeshtuh*

electricity a electricidade *eeletree-seedahd*

electricity meter o contador de electricidade *kontuh-dor deeletree-seedahd*

electric razor a máquina de barbear *makinuh duh barb-yar*

embassy a embaixada *aym-by-shah-duh*

emergency a emergência *eemer-jenss-yuh*

empty vazio(a) *vazee-oo(uh)*

end o fim *feeng*

engaged *(to be married)* casado(a) *kazah-doo(uh)*; *(phone, toilet)* ocupado(a) *oh-koopah-doo(uh)*

engine o motor *mootor*

England a Inglaterra *eengluh-terruh*

English inglês (inglesa) *eenglaysh (eenglezuh)*

enjoy: to enjoy oneself divertir-se *deever-teer-suh*; **I enjoy swimming** gosto de nadar *goshtoo duh nadar*

enough bastante *bashtant*

enquiry desk as informações *eenfoormuh-soynsh*

entertainment a diversão *deever-sowng*

entrance a entrada *ayntrah-duh*

entrance fee o bilhete de entrada *beel-yet dayn-trah-duh*

envelope o envelope *aymvuh-lop*

equipment o equipamento *eekeepuh-mentoo*

escalator a escada rolante *shkah-duh roolant*

especially especialmente *shpuss-yal-ment*

essential essencial *eesenss-yal*

Eurocheque o Eurocheque *ay-oorooshek*

Europe a Europa *ay-ooropuh*

evening a noite *noyt*; **in the evening** à noite *a noyt*

evening meal o jantar *jantar*

every cada *kah-duh*

everyone toda a gente *toh-duh uh jent*

everything todas as coisas *toh-duz ush koy-zush*

excellent excelente *eesh-suh-lent*

except excepto *eesh-setoo*

excess luggage o excesso de bagagem *eesh-sessoo duh bagah-jayng*

exchange[1] *n* a troca *trokuh*

exchange[2] *vb* trocar *trookar*

exchange rate o câmbio *kamb-yoo*

excursion a excursão *shkoorsowng*

excuse a desculpa *dush-koolpuh*; **excuse me!** *(sorry)* desculpe! *dush-koolp*; *(when passing)* com licença *kong lee-sensuh*

exhaust pipe o tubo de escape *tooboo dushkap*

exhibition a exposição *shpoozee-sowng*

exit a saída *suh-eeduh*

expensive caro(a) *kah-roo(uh)*

expert o/a perito(a) *pereetoo(uh)*

expire *(ticket, passport)* expirar *shpeerar*

express[1] *n (train)* o rápido *rapidoo*

express[2] *adj (parcel etc)* expresso *eesh-pressoo*

extra *(spare)* sobresselente *sobruh-selent*; *(more)* mais *mysh*

eye o olho *ohl-yoo*

eyeliner o eye liner *eye liner*

eye shadow a sombra *sombruh*

face a cara *kah-ruh*

facilities as instalações *eenshtaluh-soynsh*

faint desmaiar *duj-my-ar*

fair *(fun fair)* a feira *fay-ruh*

fall cair *ca-eer*

family a família *fameel-yuh*

famous famoso(a) *famoh-zoo(uh)*

fan *(electric)* a ventoinha *ventoo-een-yuh*

fan belt a correia da ventoinha *koo-rayuh duh ventoo-een-yuh*

far longe *lonj*

fare o bilhete *beel-yet*

farm a quinta *keentuh*

fast rápido(a) *rapidoo(uh)*

fat gordo(a) *gordoo(uh)*

father o pai *py*

fault *(defect)* o defeito *duh-fay-too*;
it's not my fault a culpa não é
minha *uh koolpuh nowng e meen-
yuh*

favourite favorito(a) *favoo-
reetoo(uh)*

feed alimentar *alee-mentar*

feel apalpar *apalpar*; **I feel sick**
tenho náuseas *ten-yoo nowz-yush*

ferry o ferry-boat *ferry-boat*

festival o festival *fushtee-val*

fetch *(bring)* trazer *trazehr*; *(go and
get)* ir buscar *eer booshkar*

fever a febre *februh*

few poucos(as) *poh-koosh(ush)*; **a
few** alguns (algumas) *algoonsh
(algoomush)*

fiancé(e) o/a noivo(a) *noy-voo(uh)*

field o campo *kampoo*

fill encher *enshehr*; **to fill up**
(container) encher *enshehr*; **fill it
up!** encha o depósito! *enshuh oo
duh-pozitoo*

fillet o filete *feelet*

film o filme *feelm*

filter o filtro *feeltroo*

filter-tipped com filtro *kong feeltroo*

finish acabar *akuh-bar*

fire o fogo *foh-goo*

fire brigade os bombeiros *bombay-
roosh*

fire extinguisher o extintor
shteentor

fireworks o fogo de artifício *foh-
goo dartee-feess-yoo*

first o/a primeiro(a) *preemay-roo(uh)*

first aid os primeiros socorros
preemay-roosh sookorroosh

first class de primeira classe *duh
preemay-ruh klass*

first floor o primeiro andar
preemay-ruh andar

first name o nome próprio *nom
propree-oo*

fish¹ *n* o peixe *paysh*

fish² *vb* pescar *pushkar*

fit¹ *vb* : **it doesn't fit me** não me fica
bem *nowng muh feekuh bayng*

fit² *n* *(medical)* o ataque *atak*

fix reparar *ruh-parar*

fizzy gasoso(a) *gazoh-zoo(uh)*

flash o flash *flash*

flask o termo *tehrmoo*

flat *(apartment)* o apartamento
apartuh-mentoo

flat tyre o furo *fooroo*

flight o voo *voh-oo*

flippers as barbatanas *barbuh-tah-
nush*

floor *(of building)* o andar *andar*; *(of
room)* a chão *showng*

flour a farinha *fareen-yuh*

flower a flor *flor*

flu a gripe *greep*

fly *(insect)* a mosca *moshkuh*

fly sheet o tecto duplo *tetoo
dooploo*

foggy enevoado(a) *eenuv-wah-
doo(uh)*

follow seguir *suh-geer*

food a comida *koomeeduh*

food poisoning a intoxicação alimentar *eentoxee-ka***sowng** *alee-men***tar**

foot o pé *pe*; *(measure) see* **CONVERSION CHARTS**

football o futebol *footbol*

for *(in exchange for)* para *paruh*

foreign estrangeiro(a) *shtran-**jay**-roo(uh)*

forest a floresta *floo**resh**tuh*

forget esquecer-se de *shkuh-**sehr**-suh duh*

fork o garfo *garfoo*; *(in road)* a bifurcação *beefoorkuh-**sowng***

fortnight a quinzena *keen-**zen**uh*

fountain a fonte *font*

France a França *fran***suh**

free *(not occupied)* livre *leevruh*; *(costing nothing)* grátis *grah-teesh*

freezer o congelador *konjuh-luh-**dor***

French francês (francesa) *fran***sesh** *(fran-**say**-zuh)*

French beans o feijão-verde *fay-jowng-**vehrd***

frequent frequente *fruh-**kwent***

fresh fresco(a) *fresh***koo**(uh)

fridge o frigorífico *freegoo-**ree**fikoo*

fried frito(a) *free***too**(uh)

friend o/a amigo(a) *a**mee**goo(uh)*

from de *duh*

front a frente *frent*

frozen *(food)* congelado(a) *konjuh-**lah**-doo(uh)*

fruit a fruta *froo***tuh**

fruit juice o sumo de frutas *soo***moo** duh *froo***tush**

fruit salad a salada de frutas *salah-* duh duh *froo***tush**

frying pan a frigideira *freejee-**day**-ruh*

fuel o combustível *komboosh-**tee**vel*

fuel pump a bomba de gasolina *bom**buh** duh *gazoo-**lee**nuh*

full cheio(a) *shay***oo**(uh)

full board a pensão completa *pen***sowng** *kom**plet**uh*

funny *(amusing)* engraçado(a) *ayn-grasah-doo(uh)*; *(strange)* estranho(a) *shtrahn-**yoo**-o(uh)*

fur a pele *pel*

fuse o fusível *foo***zee**vel*

gallery o museu *moo**zay**-oo*

gallon *see* **CONVERSION CHARTS**

gambling o jogo *joh-goo*

game o jogo *joh-goo*

garage a garagem *garah-**jayng***

garden o jardim *jar**deeng***

garlic o alho *al-yoo*

gas o gás *gash*

gas cylinder a botija de gás *bootee-juh* duh *gash*

gear a velocidade *vuh-loossee-**dahd***

gentleman o cavalheiro *kaval-**yay**-roo*

Gents' Homens *o**maynsh***

genuine *(leather, silver)* genuíno(a) *jun-**wee**noo(uh)*; *(antique, picture)* autêntico(a) *ow-**tent**ikoo*

German alemão (alemã) *aluh-**mowng** (aluh-**mang**)*

German measles a rubéola *roobay-ooluh*

Germany a Alemanha *aluh-**mahn**-yuh*

get *(obtain)* obter *obtehr; (receive)* receber *ruhsuhbehr; (fetch)* ir buscar *eer booskar;* **to get into** *(vehicle)* entrar *ayntrar;* **to get off** *(bus, etc)* descer de *dush-sehr duh*

gift o presente *pruh-zent*

gift shop a loja de lembranças *lojuh du laym-bransush*

gin o gin *jeen*

ginger o gengibre *jen-jeebruh*

girl a rapariga *ruh-puh-reeguh*

girlfriend a namorada *namoo-rah-duh*

give: to give back devolver *duh-volvehr*

glass *(for drinking)* o copo *kopoo; (substance)* o vidro *veedroo*

glasses os óculos *okooloosh*

gloves as luvas *loovush*

glucose a glucose *glookoz*

glue a cola *koluh*

go ir *eer;* **to go back** voltar *voltar;* **to go down** *(downstairs etc)* descer *dush-sehr;* **to go in** entrar *ayntrar;* **to go out** *(leave)* sair *sa-eer*

goggles os óculos de protecção *okooloos duh proo-tesowng*

gold o ouro *oh-roo*

golf o golfe *golf*

golf course o campo de golfe *kampoo duh golf*

good bom (boa) *bong (boh-uh)*

good afternoon boa tarde *boh-uh tard*

goodbye adeus *aday-oosh*

good evening boa noite *boh-uh noyt*

good morning bom dia *bong dee-uh*

good night boa noite *boh-uh noyt*

goose o ganso *gansoo*

gramme o grama *grah-muh*

grandfather o avô *avoh*

grandmother a avó *avo*

grapefruit a toranja *tooran-juh*

grapefruit juice o sumo de toranja *soomoo duh tooran-juh*

grapes as uvas *oovush*

grass a erva *ehrvuh*

greasy oleoso(a) *ol-yoh-zoo(uh)*

green verde *vehrd*

green card a carta verde *kartuh vehrd*

grey cinzento(a) *seen-zentoo(uh)*

grilled grelhado(a) *grel-yah-doo(uh)*

grocer's a mercearia *mersee-uh-ree-uh*

ground a terra *terruh*

ground floor o rés-do-chão *resh-doo-showng*

groundsheet o pano de chão de tenda *pah-noo duh showng duh ten-duh*

group o grupo *groopoo*

guarantee a garantia *garan-tee-uh*

guard *(on train)* o guarda *gwarduh*

guest *(house guest)* o/a convidado(a) *komvee-dah-doo(uh); (in hotel)* o/a hóspede *oshped*

guesthouse a pensão *pensowng*

guide[1] *n* o/a guia *ghee-uh*

guide[2] *vb* guiar *ghee-ar*

guidebook o roteiro *rootay-roo*

guided tour a excursão guiada *shkoor-sowng ghee-ah-duh*

gym shoes os ténis *tay-neesh*

haemorrhoids as hemorróidas *emoo-roy-dush*

hair o cabelo *kabay-loo*

hairbrush a escova de cabelo *shkovuh duh kabay-loo*

haircut o corte de cabelo *kort duh kabay-loo*

hairdresser o/a cabeleireiro(a) *kuh-buh-lay-ray-roo(uh)*

hair dryer o secador de cabelo *sekuh-dor duh kabay-loo*

hairgrip o gancho de cabelo *ganshoo duh kabay-loo*

hair spray o spray para o cabelo *shpry pro kabay-loo*

half a metade *muh-tahd*; **a half bottle of** meia garrafa de *mayuh garah-fuh duh*

half board a meia pensão *mayuh pensowng*

half fare o meio bilhete *mayoo beel-yet*

ham o presunto *pruh-zoontoo*

hand a mão *mowng*

handbag o saco de mão *sah-koo duh mowng*

handicapped deficiente *duh-feess-yent*

handkerchief o lenço *lensoo*

hand luggage a bagagem de mão *bagah-jayng duh mowng*

hand-made feito(a) à mão *fay-too(uh) a mowng*

hangover a ressaca *resah-kuh*

happen acontecer *akontuh-sehr*; **what happened?** o que aconteceu? *oo kee akontuh-say-oo*

happy feliz *fuh-leesh*

harbour o porto *portoo*

hard duro(a) *dooroo(uh)*

hat o chapéu *shapay-oo*

have ter *tehr*; *see* **GRAMMAR**

hay fever a febre dos fenos *februh doosh fay-noosh*

hazelnut a avelã *avuh-lang*

he ele *ayl*; *see* **GRAMMAR**

head a cabeça *kabay-suh*

headache a dor de cabeça *dor duh kabay-suh*

hear ouvir *oh-veer*

heart o coração *kooruh-sowng*

heart attack o ataque de coração *atak duh kooruh-sowng*

heater o aquecedor *akussuh-dor*

heating o aquecimento *akussee-mentoo*

heavy pesado(a) *puh-zah-doo(uh)*

hello olá *oh-la*; *(on telephone)* está? *shta*

help¹ *n* a ajuda *ajooduh*; **help!** socorro! *sookorroo*

help² *vb* ajudar *ajoodar*; **can you help me?** pode-me ajudar? *pod-muh ajoodar*

herb a erva *ehrvuh*

here aqui *akee*

high alto(a) *altoo(uh)*

high blood pressure a tensão alta *tensowng altuh*

highchair a cadeira de bebé *kaday-ruh duh bebe*

high tide a maré-cheia *mare-shayuh*

hill a colina *koolenuh*

hill-walking o montanhismo *montan-yeej-moo*

hire alugar *aloogar*

hit atingir *ateen-jeer*

hitchhike andar à boleia *andar a boolayuh*

hold segurar *suh-goorar*; *(contain)* conter *contehr*

hold-up *(traffic jam)* o engarrafamento *ayn-garrah-fuh-mentoo*

hole o buraco *boorah-koo*

holiday o feriado *fuh-re-ahdoo*; **on holiday** em férias *ayng fehr-yush*

home a casa *kah-zuh*

homesick: to be homesick ter saudades *tehr sow-dah-dush*

honey o mel *mel*

honeymoon a lua-de-mel *loo-uh duh mel*

hope esperar *shpuh-rar*; **I hope so/not** espero que sim/não *shpehroo kuh seeng/nowng*

hors d'oeuvre a entrada *ayn-trah-duh*

horse o cavalo *kavah-loo*

hose o tubo *tooboo*

hospital o hospital *oshpee-tal*

hot quente *kent*; **I'm hot** tenho calor *ten-yoo kalor*; **it's hot** *(weather)* está calor *shta kalor*

hotel o hotel *oh-tel*

hour a hora *oruh*

house a casa *kah-zuh*

house wine o vinho da casa *veen-yoo duh kah-zuh*

hovercraft o hovercraft *hovercraft*

how *(in what way)* como *koh-moo*; **how much?** quanto? *kwantoo*; **how many?** quantos(as)? *kwantoosh(ush)*; **how are you?** como está? *koh-moo shta*

hungry: I am hungry tenho fome *ten-yoo fom*

hurry: I'm in a hurry tenho pressa *ten-yoo pressuh*

hurt doer *doo-er*; **that hurts** isso dói *eesoo doy*

husband o marido *mareedoo*

I eu *ay-oo*; see **GRAMMAR**

ice o gelo *jay-loo*

ice cream o gelado *juh-lah-doo*

iced gelado(a) *juh-lah-doo(uh)*

ice lolly o gelado *juh-lah-doo*

if se *suh*

ignition a ignição *eegnee-sowng*

ill doente *doo-ent*

immediately imediatamente *eemudee-ah-tuh-ment*

important importante *eempoor-tant*

impossible impossível *eempoo-seevel*

in dentro de *dentroo duh*

inch a polegada *pool-gah-duh*; see **CONVERSION CHARTS**

included incluído(a) *een-klwee-doo(uh)*

indigestion a indigestão *eendee-jesh-towng*

indoors em casa *ayng kah-zuh*

infectious infeccioso(a) *eemfess-yoh-zoo(uh)*

information a informação *eemfoormuh-sowng*

information office as informações *eemformuh-soynsh*

injection a injecção *eenjesowng*

injured ferido(a) *fereedoo(uh)*

ink a tinta *teentuh*

insect o insecto *eensetoo*

insect bite a mordedura de insecto *moorduh-**door**uh deen-**set**oo*
insect repellent o repelente *ruh-puh-**lent***
inside o interior *eentuh-ree-**or***
instant coffee o café instantâneo *kuh-**fe** eenshtan-**tahn**-yoo*
instead em vez disso *aym vesh **dee**soo*
instructor o/a instrutor(a) *eenshtroo**tor**(uh)*
insulin a insulina *eensoo-**lee**nuh*
insurance o seguro *suh-**goo**roo*
insurance certificate a apólice de seguro *a**pol**eess duh suh-**goo**roo*
interesting interessante *eentuh-re-**sant***
international internacional *eenter-nass-**yoo**nal*
interpreter o/a intérprete *eentehr-**pret***
into em *ayng*
invitation o convite *kom**veet***
invite convidar *komvee**dar***
invoice a factura *fak**too**ruh*
Ireland a Irlanda *eer**lan**duh*
Irish irlandês (irlandesa) *eerlan-**desh** (eerlan-**day**-zuh)*
iron (for clothes) o ferro *fer**roo***
ironmonger's a loja de ferragens *loj**uh duh fe**rah**-jaynsh*
is see GRAMMAR
island a ilha *eel-**yuh***
it o/a *oo/uh; see* GRAMMAR
Italian italiano(a) *eetal-**yah**-noo(uh)*
Italy a Itália *eetal-**yuh***
itch a comichão *koomee-**showng***

jack (for car) o macaco *ma**kah**-koo*
jacket o casaco *ka**zah**-koo*
jam (food) a compota *kom**pot**uh*
jammed bloqueado(a) *blook-**yah**-doo(uh)*
jar (container) o jarro *jar**roo***
jazz o jazz *jaz*
jeans as jeans *jeans*
jelly (dessert) a geleia *juh-**lay**uh*
jellyfish a medusa *muh-**doo**zuh*
jersey o pulover *poo**loh**-vehr*
jeweller's a joalharia *jwal-yuh-**ree**-uh*
jewellery a joalharia *jwal-yuh-**ree**-uh*
Jewish judeu (judia) *joo**day**-oo (joo**dee**-uh)*
job o emprego *aym-**pray**-goo*
jog: to go jogging ir fazer jogging *eer fa**zehr** jogging*
joke a anedota *anuh-**dot**uh*
journey a viagem *vee-**ah**-jayng*
jug o jarro *jar**roo***
juice o sumo *soo**moo***
jump leads os cabos de emergência *kah-boosh deemer-**jenss**-yuh*
junction a bifurcação *beefoorkuh-**sowng**; (crossroads) o cruzamento *kroozuh-**men**too*
just: just two apenas dois *a**pay**-nush doysh*; **I've just arrived** acabo de chegar *a**kah**-boo duh shuh-**gar***

keep (retain) guardar *gwar**dar***
kettle a chaleira *sha**lay**-ruh*
key a chave *shahv*
kidneys (as food) os rins *reensh*

kilo o quilo *keeloo*

kilometre o quilómetro *kee-lometroo*

kind[1] *n (sort, type)* a espécie *shpessee*

kind[2] *adj (person)* amável *amah-vel*

kiss beijar *bay-jar*

kitchen a cozinha *koozeen-yuh*

knife a faca *fah-kuh*

know *(facts)* saber *sabehr*; *(be acquainted with)* conhecer *koon-yuh-sehr*

lace *(of shoe)* a renda *renduh*

ladder a escada *shkah-duh*

Ladies' Senhoras *sun-yorush*

lady a senhora *sun-yoru*

lager a cerveja *servay-juh*

lake o lago *lah-goo*

lamb o cordeiro *koor-day-roo*

lamp o candeeiro *kandee-ay-roo*

lane a travessa *travessuh*; *(of motorway)* a faixa *fy-shuh*

language a língua *leengwuh*

large grande *grand*

last último(a) *ooltimoo(uh)*; **last week** na semana passada *nuh semah-nuh puh-sah-duh*

late tarde *tard*; **the train is late** a comboio está atrasado *oo komboyoo shta atruh-zah-doo*; **sorry we are late** desculpe o atraso *dush-koolp oo atrah-zoo*

later mais tarde *mysh tard*

launderette a lavandaria automática *lavanduh-ree-uh owtoo-matikoo*

laundry service o serviço de lavandaria *ser-veesoo duh lavanduh-ree-uh*

lavatory o lavabo *lavah-boo*

lawyer o advogado *advoogah-doo*

laxative o laxativo *lashuh-teevoo*

lay-by o desvio para estacionamento *duj-vee-oo paruh shtass-yoonuh-mentoo*

lead *(electric)* o cabo *kah-boo*

leader *(guide)* o guia *ghee-uh*

leak *(of gas, liquid)* a fuga *fooguh*; *(in roof)* a goteira *goo-tay-ruh*

learn aprender *aprendehr*

least: at least pelo meno *peloo may-noosh*

leather o couro *koh-roo*

leave partir *perteer*; *(leave behind)* deixar *day-shar*; **when does the train leave?** a que horas parte o comboio? *uh kee orush part oo komboyoo*

leeks os alhos-porros *al-yoosh-porroosh*

left: (on/to the) left à esquerda *a shkehrduh*

left-luggage (office) o depósito de bagagens *duh-pozitoo duh bagah-jaynsh*

leg a perna *pehrnuh*

lemon o limão *leemowng*

lemonade a limonada *leemoo-nah-duh*

lemon tea o carioca de limão *karee-okuh duh leemowng*

lend emprestar *aympresh-tar*

lens a lente *lent*

less menos *may-noosh*

lesson a lição *leesowng*

let *(allow)* deixar *day-shar*; *(hire out)* alugar *aloogar*

letter a carta *kartuh*

lettuce a alface *alfass*

library a biblioteca *beeblee-oo-tekuh*

licence a autorização *owtoo-reezuh-sowng*

lid a tampa *tampuh*

lie down deitar-se *day-tar-suh*

lifeboat o salva-vidas *salvuh-veedush*

lifeguard o nadador-salvador *naduh-dor-salvuh-dor*

life jacket o colete de salvação *koolet duh salvuh-sowng*

lift o elevador *eeluh-vuh-dor*

light a luz *loosh*; **have you got a light?** tem lume? *tayng loom*

light bulb a lâmpada *lahm-paduh*

lighter o isqueiro *eeshkay-roo*

like¹ *prep* como *koh-moo*; **like this** assim *aseeng*

like² *vb* gostar de *gooshtar duh*; **I like coffee** gosto do café *goshtoo doo kuh-fe*

lime *(fruit)* a lima *leemuh*

line a linha *leen-yuh*

lip salve a manteiga de cacao *mantay-guh duh kakow*

lipstick o bâton *bah-tong*

liqueur o licor *leekor*

listen (to) ouvir *oh-veer*

litre o litro *leetroo*

little: a little milk um pouco de leite *oom pohkoo duh layt*

live viver *veevehr*; **he lives in London** el vive em Londres *ayl veev ayng*

londrush

liver o fígado *feeguh-doo*

living room a sala de estar *sah-luh dushtar*

loaf o pão *powng*

lobster a lagosta *lagoshtuh*

local *(wine, speciality)* local *lookal*

lock¹ *vb* *(door)* fechar com chave *fushar kong shav*

lock² *n* *(on door, box)* a fechadura *feshuh-dooruh*

lollipop o chupa-chupa *shoopuh-shoopuh*

London Londres *londrush*

long comprido(a) *kom-preedoo(uh)*; **for a long time** durante muito tempo *doorant mweentoo tempoo*

look olhar *ohl-yar*; *(seem)* parecer *paruh-sehr*; **to look after** cuidar de *kweedar duh*; **to look for** procurar *prookoorar*

lorry o camião *kam-yowng*

lose perder *perdehr*

lost *(object)* perdido(a) *perdeedoo(uh)*; **I have lost my wallet** perdi o meu cartão *perdee oo may-oo kartowng*; **I am lost** perdi-me *perdee-muh*

lost property office a secção de perdidos e achados *seksowng duh perdeedooz ee ashah-doosh*

lot: a lot muitos *mweentoosh*

lotion a loção *loosowng*

loud alto(a) *altoo(uh)*

lounge *(in hotel)* a sala de estar *sah-luh dushtar*

love *(person)* amar *uh-mar*; **I love swimming** gosto muito de nadar *goshtoo mweentoo duh nadar*

lovely encantador(a) *aynkantuh-dor(uh)*

low baixo(a) *by-shoo(uh)*

low tide a maré-baixa *mare-by-shuh*

lucky afortunado *afortoo-nah-doo*

luggage a bagagem *bagah-jayng*

luggage allowance o limite de peso autorizado *leemeet duh pay-zoo owtooree-zah-doo*

luggage rack (on car, in train) o porta-bagagens *portuh-bagah-jaynsh*

luggage tag a etiqueta de bagagem *etee-ketuh duh bagah-jayng*

luggage trolley o carrinho para a bagagem *kareen-yoo pra bagah-jayng*

lunch o almoço *almoh-soo*

luxury o luxo *looshoo*

macaroni o macarrão *maka-rowng*

machine a máquina *makinuh*

madam senhora *sun-yoruh*

magazine a revista *ruh-veeshtuh*

maid (in hotel) a empregada *aympruh-gah-duh*

main principal *preenseepal*

main course o prato principal *prah-too preensee-pal*

mains (electric) o quadro da electricidade *kwadro duh eeletree-see-dahd*

make (generally) fazer *fazehr*; (meal) preparar *pruh-parar*

make-up a maquilhagem *makeel-yah-jayng*

mallet o maço *mah-soo*

man o homem *omayng*

manager o gerente *juh-rent*

many muitos(as) *mweentoosh(ush)*

map o mapa *mah-puh*

margarine a margarina *marguh-reenuh*

market o mercado *merkah-doo*

marmalade o doce de laranja *dohss duh laranjuh*

married casado(a) *kazah-doo(uh)*

marzipan o maçapão *massuh-powng*

mascara o rímel ® *reemel*

mass (in church) a missa *meessuh*

match o fósforo *fosh-fooroo*

material (cloth) o material *matuh-ree-al*

matter: it doesn't matter não tem importância *nowng tayng eempoor-tanss-yuh*

mayonnaise a maionese *myoo-nez*

meal a refeição *ruh-fay-sowng*

mean (signify) significar *seegnee-feekar*; **what does this mean?** o que isto significa? *o kee eeshtoo seegnee-feekuh*

measles o sarampo *sarampo*

meat a carne *karn*

mechanic o mecânico *mekah-nikoo*

medicine o medicamento *medeekuh-mentoo*

medium médio(a) *med-yoo(uh)*

medium rare médio(a) *med-yoo(uh)*

meet encontrar *aynkon-trar*

melon a melão *melowng*

melt fundir *foondeer*

member (of club etc) o sócio *soss-yoo*

men os homens *omaynsh*

menu a ementa *eementuh*

meringue o merengue *muh-renguh*

message a mensagem *mensah-jayng*

metal o metal *muh-tal*

meter o contador *kontuh-dor*

metre o metro *metroo*

migraine a enxaqueca *aynshuh-kekuh*

mile *see* CONVERSION CHARTS

milk o leite *layt*

milk shake o batido de leite *bateedoo duh layt*

millimetre o milímetro *mee-leemetroo*

million o milhão *meel-yowng*

mince a carne picada *karn peekah-duh*

mind: do you mind if I...? importa-se que eu ...? *eemportuh-suh kee ay-oo ...*

mineral water a água mineral *ahg-wuh meenuh-ral*

minimum o mínimo *meenimoo*

minister *(church)* o pastor *pashtor*

minor road a estrada secundária *shtrah-duh sekoon-dar-yuh*

mint *(herb)* a hortelã *ortuh-lang*; *(sweet)* a pastilha de mentol *pash-teel-yuh duh mentol*

minute o minuto *meenootoo*

mirror o espelho *shpel-yoo*

miss *(train, etc)* perder *perdehr*

Miss Menina *muh-neenuh*

missing: my son is missing não encontro a meu filho *nowng ayng-kontroo oo may-oo feel-yoo*

mistake o erro *erroo*

misty enevoado(a) *eenuv-wah-doo(uh)*

misunderstanding: there's been a misunderstanding houve um mal-entendido *ohv oom mal-enten-deedoo*

modern moderno(a) *moodehrnoo(uh)*

moisturizer o creme hidratante *krem eedruh-tant*

monastery o mosteiro *moosh-tay-roo*

money o dinheiro *deen-yay-roo*

money order o vale postal *vahl pooshtal*

month o mês *mesh*

monument o monumento *moonoo-mentoo*

mop *(for floor)* a esfregona *shfregonuh*

more mais *mysh*; **more than three** mais de três *mysh duh tresh*; **more bread** mais pão *mysh powng*

morning a manhã *man-yang*

mosquito o mosquito *moosh-keetoo*

mother a mãe *myng*

motor o motor *mootor*

motorboat o barco a motor *barkoo uh mootor*

motorcycle a motocicleta *mootoosee-kletuh*

motorway a auto-estrada *owtoo-shtrah-duh*

mountain a montanha *montahn-yuh*

mousse a mousse *mooss*

mouth a boca *boh-kuh*

Mr Senhor *sun-yor*

Mrs Senhora *sun-yoruh*

much muito(a) *mweentoo(uh)*; **too**

much demais *duh-mysh*
mumps a papeira *papay-ruh*
museum o museu *moozay-oo*
mushroom o cogumelo *koogoo-meloo*
music a música *moozikuh*
mussel o mexilhão *musheel-yowng*
must dever *devehr*
mustard a mostardo *moosh-tarduh*
mutton o carneiro *karnay-roo*

nail *(metal)* o prego *pray-goo*
nail polish o verniz das unhas *verneesh duz oon-yush*
nail polish remover a acetona *assuh-tonuh*
naked nu(a) *noo(uh)*
name o nome *nom*
napkin o guardanapo *gwarduh-nah-poo*
nappy a fralda *fralduh*
narrow estreito(a) *shtray-too(uh)*
nationality a nacionalidade *nass-yoonalee-dahd*
navy blue azul marinho a*zool mareen-yoo*
near perto *pehrtoo*
necessary necessário(a) *nussuh-sar-yoo(uh)*
neck o pesoço *push-koh-soo*
necklace o colar *koolar*
need: I need an aspirin preciso duma aspirina *pre-seezoo doomuh ashpee-reenuh*
needle a agulha *agool-yuh*; **a needle and thread** uma agulha e a linha *oomuh agool-yuh ee uh leen-yuh*

negative *(photography)* o negativo *nuh-guh-teevoo*
neighbour o/a vizinho(a) *veezeen-yoo(uh)*
never nunca *noonkuh*; **I never drink wine** nunca bebo vinho *noonkuh beboo veen-yoo*
new novo(a) *noh-voo(uh)*
news a notícia *noo-teess-yuh*
newsagent a tabacaria *tabuh-kuh-ree-uh*
newspaper o jornal *joornal*
New Year o Ano Novo *ahnoo noh-voo*
New Zealand a Nova Zelândia *novuh zuh-landee-uh*
next próximo(a) *prossimoo(uh)*
nice simpático(a) *seem-patikoo(uh)*
night a noite *noyt*
nightclub a boite *bwat*
nightdress a camisa de noite *kameezuh duh noyt*
no não *nowng*; **no thank you** não, obrigado *nowng oh-breegah-doo*
nobody ninguém *neengayng*
noisy barulhento(a) *barool-yentoo(uh)*
nonalcoholic não-alcoólico(a) *nowng-alk-wolikoo(uh)*
none nenhum(a) *nun-yoom(uh)*; **there's none left** não sobrou nada *nowng soobroh nahduh*
non smoking *(compartment)* para não fumadores *paruh nowng-foomuh-dorush*
north o norte *nort*
Northern Ireland a Irlanda do Norte *eer-landuh doo nort*

not não *nowng*; **I don't know** não sei *nowng say*

note a nota *notuh*

note pad o bloco de apontamentos *blokoo dapontuh-mentoosh*

nothing nada *nah-duh*

now agora *agoruh*

number o número *noomeroo*

nurse a enfermeira *aymfer-may-ruh*

nut *(to eat)* a noz *nosh*; *(for bolt)* a porca *porkuh*

occasionally às vezes *ash vay-zush*

of de *duh*

off *(machine etc)* desligado(a) *duj-leegah-doo(uh)*; *(rotten)* pôdre *poh-druh*

offer oferecer *of-fuh-ruh-sehr*

office o escritório *shkree-tor-yoo*

often muitas vezes *mweentush vay-zush*

oil o óleo *ol-yoo*

oil filter o filtro do óleo *feeltroo doo ol-yoo*

ointment a pomada *poo-mah-duh*

OK está bem *shta bayng*

old velho(a) *vel-yoo(uh)*; **how old are you?** que idade tem? *kuh eedahd tayng*

olive a azeitona *azay-tonuh*

olive oil o azeite *azayt*

omelette a omeleta *omuh-letuh*

on *(light, engine)* aceso(a) *asay-zoo(uh)*; **on (the table)** na (mesa) nuh *(may-zuh)*

once uma vez *oomuh vesh*

one um (uma) *oom (oomuh)*

one-way *(street)* de sentido único *duh senteedoo oonikoo*

onion a cebola *suh-boluh*

only só *so*

open[1] *adj* aberto(a) *abehrtoo(uh)*

open[2] *vb* abrir *abreer*

opera a ópera *operuh*

operator o operador *oh-peruh-dor*

opposite *(house, etc)* em frente *aym frent*

or ou *oh*

orange[1] *adj* cor de laranja *kor duh laranjuh*

orange[2] *n* a laranja *laranjuh*

orange juice o sumo de laranja *soomoo duh laranjuh*

order encomendar *aynkoo-mendar*

original original *oh-reejee-nal*

other: the other one o/a outro(a) *oo/uh oh-troo(uh)*; **do you have any others?** tem mais? *tayng mysh*

ounce a onça *onsuh*; *see* **CONVERSION CHARTS**

out *(light)* apagado(a) *apuh-gah-doo(uh)*; **he's out** ele saiu *ayl sa-yoo*

outdoor *(pool, etc)* ao ar livre *ow ar leevruh*

outside lá fora *la foruh*

oven o forno *fornoo*

over *(on top of)* sobre *soh-bruh*

overcharge cobrar demais *koobrar duh-mysh*

owe dever *devehr*; **you owe me …** deve-me … *dev-muh*

owner o dono *doh-noo*

oyster a ostra *oshtruh*

pack (luggage) fazer as malas fazehr ush mah-lush

package o embrulho aym-**brool**-yoo

package tour a viagem organizada vee-**ah**-jayng organee-**zah**-duh

packed lunch o almoço embalado almoh-soo aymba-**lah**-doo

packet o pacote pakot

paddling pool a piscina para crianças peesh-**see**nuh paruh kree-ansush

paid pago(a) **pah**-goo(uh)

painful doloroso(a) dooloo-**roh**-zoo(uh)

painkiller o analgésico anal-**jez**ikoo

painting a pintura pin**too**ruh

pair o par par

palace o palácio pa**lass**-yoo

pan a panela pa**nel**uh

pancake a panqueca pan**kek**uh

panties as cuecas **kwek**ush

pants as cuecas **kwek**ush

paper o papel puh-**pel**

paraffin a parafina paruh-**fee**nuh

parcel a encomenda aynkoo-**mend**uh

pardon (I didn't understand) desculpe? dush-**koolp**; **I beg your pardon!** como disse? koh-moo deess

parents os pais pysh

park[1] n o parque park

park[2] vb estacionar shtass-yoo**nar**

parking disc o disco de estacionamento **deesh**koo dushtass-yoonuh-**mentoo**

parsley a salsa **sal**suh

part a parte part

party (group) o grupo **groo**poo

passenger o passageiro passuh-**jay**-roo

passport o passaporte passuh-**port**

passport control o controle de passaportes kontrol duh passuh-**portsh**

pasta as massas **mass**ush

pastry a massa **mass**uh; (cake) o bolo **boh**-loo

pâté o paté pa**tay**

path o caminho ka**meen**-yoo

pay pagar pa**gar**

payment o pagamento paguh-**mentoo**

peach o pêssego **pay**-suh-goo

peanut o amendoim amendoo-**eeng**

pear a pera **pay**-ruh

peas as ervilhas ehr**veel**-yush

peel (fruit) descascar dush-kash**kar**

peg (for clothes) o cabide ka**beed**; (for tent) a mola **mol**uh

pen a caneta ka**net**uh

pencil o lápis **lah**-peesh

penicillin a penicilina puneesee-**leenuh**

penknife o canivete kaneevet

pensioner o/a reformado(a) ruh-foor**mah**-doo(uh)

pepper (spice) a pimenta pee**ment**uh; (vegetable) o pimento pee**mentoo**

per: per hour por hora poor **or**uh; **per week** por semana poor se**mah**-nuh

perfect perfeito(a) per**fay**-too(uh)

performance a representação rupruh-zentuh-**sowng**

perfume o perfume *perfoom*
perhaps talvez *talvesh*
period *(menstruation)* a menstruação *mensh-troo-uh-sowng*
perm a permanente *permuh-nent*
permit a licença *leesensuh*
person a pessoa *puh-so-uh*
petrol a gasolina *gazoo-leenuh*
petrol station a bomba de gasolina *bombuh duh gazoo-leenuh*
phone *see* **telephone**
photocopy a fotocópia *footoo-kop-yuh*
photograph a fotografia *footoogruh-fee-uh*
picnic o piquenique *peekuh-neek*
picture *(painting)* o quadro *kwadroo*; *(photo)* a fotografia *footoogruh-fee-uh*
pie o pastel *pashtel*
piece o bocado *bookah-doo*
pill o comprimido *kompree-meedoo*
pillow a almofada *almoofah-duh*
pillowcase o travesseiro *travuh-say-roo*
pin o alfinete *alfeenet*
pineapple o ananás *anuh-nash*
pink cor-de-rosa *kor-duh-rozuh*
pint *see* **CONVERSION CHARTS**; **a pint of beer** ≈ uma caneca de cerveja *kaneh-kuh duh servay-juh*
pipe o cachimbo *kasheemboo*
plane o avião *av-yowng*
plaster *(sticking plaster)* o adesivo *aduh-zeevoo*
plastic o plástico *plash-tikoo*
plate o prato *prah-too*

platform a linha *leen-yuh*
play *(games)* jogar *joogar*
playroom a sala de jogos *sah-luh duh jogoosh*
please por favor *poor favor*
pliers o alicate *aleekat*
plug *(electrical)* a ficha *feeshuh*; *(for sink)* a tampa *tampuh*
plum a ameixa *amay-shuh*
plumber o canalizador *kanaleezuh-dor*
points *(in car)* os platinados *platee-nah-doosh*
police a polícia *pooleess-yuh*
policeman o polícia *pooleess-yuh*
police station a esquadra *shkwah-druh*
polish *(for shoes)* a pomada para o calçado *poomah-duh pro kalsah-doo*
polluted poluído(a) *pool-weedoo(uh)*
pony trekking o passeio a cavalo *pasayoo uh kavah-loo*
pool *(swimming)* a piscina *peesh-seenuh*
popular popular *poopoolar*
pork a carne de porco *karn duh porkoo*
port *(seaport, wine)* o porto *portoo*
porter *(in hotel)* o porteiro *poortay-roo*; *(in station)* o carregador *karruh-guh-dor*
Portugal Portugal *portoo-gal*
Portuguese português (portuguesa) *poortoo-gaysh* (*poortoo-gay-zuh*)
possible possível *pooseevel*
post pôr no correio *pohr noo*

koorayoo

postbox o marco do correio *markoo doo koorayoo*

postcard o postal *pooshtal*

postcode o código postal *kodigoo pooshtal*

post office os correios *koorayoosh*

pot *(for cooking)* a panela *paneluh*

potato a batata *batah-tuh*

pottery a cerâmica *suh-rahmikuh*

pound *(weight, money)* a libra *leebruh*; see **CONVERSION CHARTS**

powdered milk o leite em po *layt ayng po*

pram o carrinho de bebé *kareen-yoo duh bebe*

prawn o lagostim *lagoosh-teeng*

prefer preferir *pruh-fereer*

pregnant grávida *graviduh*

prepare preparar *pruh-parar*

prescription a receita médica *ruh-say-tuh medikuh*

present *(gift)* o presente *pruh-zent*

pretty bonito(a) *booneetoo(uh)*

price o preço *pray-soo*

price list a lista de preços *leeshtuh duh pray-soosh*

priest o padre *padruh*

print *(photo)* a fotografia *footoogruh-fee-uh*

private privado(a) *preevah-doo(uh)*

probably provavelmente *proovah-velment*

problem o problema *proo-blemuh*

programme o programa *proograh-muh*

pronounce pronunciar *proonoonss-yar*; how do you pronounce this?

como se pronuncia isto? *kohmoo suh proonoon-see-uh eeshtoo*

Protestant protestante *prootush-tant*

prune a ameixa passada *amay-shuh pasah-duh*

public público(a) *pooblikoo(uh)*

public holiday o feriado *fuh-ree-ah-doo*

pudding o pudim *poodeeng*

pull puxar *pooshar*

pullover o pulover *pooloh-vehr*

puncture o furo *fooroo*

purple roxo(a) *roh-shoo(uh)*

purse a bolsa *bohlsuh*

push empurrar *aym-poorrar*

put pôr *pohr*

pyjamas o pijama *peejah-muh*

queue a bicha *beeshuh*

quick rápido(a) *rapidoo(uh)*

quickly depressa *duh-pressuh*

quiet *(place)* sossegado(a) *soosuh-gah-doo(uh)*

quilt o edredão *edruh-downg*

quite: it's quite good é bastante bom *e bashtant bong*; **it's quite expensive** é muito caro *e mweentoo kah-roo*

rabbit o coelho *koo-el-yoo*

racket a raqueta *raketuh*

radio o rádio *rahd-yoo*

radish o rabanete *rabuh-net*

railway station a estação de comboio *shtasowng duh komboyoo*

rain a chuva *shoovuh*

raincoat o impermeável *eempermee-ah-vel*

raining: it's raining está a chover *shta uh shoovehr*

raisin a passa *passuh*

rare *(unique)* raro(a) *rah-roo(uh)*; *(steak)* mal passado(a) *mal pasah-doo(uh)*

raspberry a framboesa *fram-bway-zuh*

rate a taxa *tashuh*; **rate of exchange** o câmbio *kamb-yoo*

raw cru(a) *kroo(uh)*

razor a navalha de barbear *naval-yuh duh barbee-ar*

razor blades as lâminas de barbear *lahminush duh barbee-ar*

ready pronto(a) *prontoo(uh)*

real real *ree-al*

receipt o recibo *ruh-seeboo*

recently há pouco *ah poh-koo*

reception (desk) a recepção *ruh-sepsowng*

recipe a receita *ruh-saytuh*

recommend recomendar *ruh-koomendar*

record *(music, etc)* o disco *deeshkoo*

red vermelho(a) *vermel-yoo(uh)*

reduction o desconto *dush-kontoo*

refill *(for pen, for lighter)* a carga *karguh*

refund o reembolso *ree-aym-bolsoo*

registered registado(a) *rujeesh-tah-doo(uh)*

regulations os regulamentos *ruh-gooluh-mentoosh*

reimburse reembolsar *ree-aym-bolsar*

relation *(family)* o parente *parent*

relax repousar *ruh-poh-zar*

reliable *(company, service)* de confiança *duh komfee-ansuh*

remain ficar *feekar*

remember lembrar-se de *laym-brar-suh duh*

rent *(house, car)* alugar *aloogar*

rental *(house, car)* o aluguer *aloogehr*

repair reparar *ruh-parar*

repeat repetir *ruh-puh-teer*

reservation a reserva *ruh-zehrvuh*

reserve reservar *ruh-zervar*

reserved reservado(a) *ruh-zervah-doo(uh)*

rest[1] *n* *(repose)* o descanso *dush-kansoo*; **the rest of the wine** o resto do vinho *oo reshtoo doo veen-yoo*

rest[2] *vb* descansar *dush-kansar*

restaurant o restaurante *rushtoh-rant*

restaurant car o vagão restaurant *vagowng rushtoh-rant*

return *(go back)* voltar *voltar*; *(give back)* devolver *duh-volvehr*

return ticket o bilhete de ida e volta *beel-yet duh eeduh ee voltuh*

reverse-charge call a chamada pagável no destino *shamah-duh pagah-vel noo dush-teenoo*

rheumatism o reumatismo *rayoomuh-teej-moo*

rhubarb o ruibarbo *rwee-barboo*

rice o arroz *arosh*

ride *(on horse)* montar a cavalo *montar uh kavah-loo*

right[1] *adj* *(correct)* certo(a) *sehrtoo(uh)*

right² adv : **(on/to the) right** à direita
  a dee**ray**-tuh
ring o anel a*nel*
ripe maduro(a) ma**doo**roo(uh)
river o rio *ree-oo*
road a estrada *shtrah-duh*
road map o mapa das estradas
  mah-puh dush shtrah-dush
roast assado(a) a*sah*-doo(uh)
roll (bread) o papo-seco pah-poo-
  say-koo
roof o telhado *tul-yah-doo*
roof rack o tejadilho *tejuh-deel-yoo*
room (in house, hotel) o quarto
  kwartoo; (space) o espaço **shpah**-
  soo
room service o serviço de quarto
  ser**vee**soo duh **kwar**too
rope a corda *kor*duh
rosé o vinho rosé *veen-*yoo roh-*zay*
rough (sea) bravo(a) *brah*-voo(uh)
round redondo(a) ruh-**don**doo(uh)
route a rota *roo*tuh
rowing boat o barco a remos
  *bar*koo uh *ray-*moosh
rubber a borracha *boo*rah-shuh
rubber band o elástico ee*lash-tik*oo
rubbish o lixo *lee*shoo
rucksack a mochila *moo*sheeluh
rum o rum *roong*
rush hour a hora de ponta *o*ruh duh
  *pon*tuh

safe¹ n o cofre **kof**ruh
safe² adj (beach, medicine) seguro(a)
  suh-**goo**roo(uh)
safety pin o alfinete de segurança

  al**fee**net duh suh-goo*ran*-suh
sail a vela *vel*uh
sailboard a prancha **pran**shuh
sailing (sport) a vela *vel*uh
salad a salada *sal*ah-duh
salad dressing o tempero para a
  salada *tem*pay-roo pra sa*lah*-duh
salmon o salmão *sal*mowng
salt o sal *sal*
same mesmo(a) **mej**-moo(uh)
sand a areia a*ray*-uh
sandals as sandálias san**dahl**-yush
sandwich a sanduíche sand-**weesh**
sanitary towel o penso higiénico
  *pen*soo eej-*yen*ikoo
sardine a sardinha sar**deen**-yuh
sauce o molho **mohl**-yoo
saucepan a caçarola *kassuh-rol*uh
saucer o pires *pee*rush
sauna a sauna *sow*-nuh
sausage a salsicha *sal*see-shuh
savoury (not sweet) saboroso(a)
  saboo-roh-zoo(uh)
say dizer dee*zehr*
scarf (long) o cachecol *kashuh-kol*;
  (square) o lenço (de pescoço)
  *len*soo (duh push-*koh-soo*)
school a escola *shkol*uh
scissors a tesoura tuh-**zoh**-ruh
Scotch o whisky **weesh**kee
Scotland a Escócia **shkoss**-yuh
Scottish escocês (escocesa)
  shkoosesh (*shkoosay-zuh*)
screw o parafuso *paruh-***foo**zoo
screwdriver a chave de parafusos
  *shahv duh paruh-***foo**zoosh
sculpture (object) a escultura

shkool-**too**ruh

sea o mar *mar*

seafood o marisco *ma**reesh**koo*

seasickness o enjoo *enjoh-oo*

seaside a praia *pry-uh*

season ticket o passe *pass*

seat *(chair)* a cadeira *ka**day**-ruh*; *(in train, theatre)* o lugar *loo**gar***

second segundo(a) *suh-**goon**doo(uh)*

second class de segunda classe *duh suh-**goon**duh klass*

see ver *vehr*

self-service o self-service *self-service*

sell vender *ven**dehr***

Sellotape ® a fita-cola *feetuh-**kol**uh*

send mandar *man**dar***

senior citizen o/a reformado(a) *ruh-foor**mah**-doo(uh)*

separate separado(a) *suh-parah-doo(uh)*

serious grave *grahv*

serve servir *ser**veer***

service *(in restaurant)* o serviço *ser**vee**soo*

service charge o serviço *ser**vee**soo*

set menu a refeição da casa *ruh-fay-**sowng** duh **kah**-zuh*

shade o tom *tong*

shallow pouco profundo(a) *poh-koo proo-**foon**doo(uh)*

shampoo o champô *sham**poh***

shampoo and set a lavagem e mise *la**vah**-jayng ee meez*

shandy a cerveja e limonada *ser**vay**-juh ee leemoo-**nah**-duh*

share repartir *ruh-par**teer***

shave fazer a barba *fa**zehr uh** barbuh*

shaving cream o creme de barbear *krem duh barbee-**ar***

she ela *eluh*; *see* GRAMMAR

sheet o lençol *len**sol***

shellfish o marisco *ma**reesh**koo*

sherry o xerez *shuh-**resh***

ship o barco *bar**koo***

shirt a camisa *ka**mee**zuh*

shock absorber o amortecedor *amortuh-suh-**dor***

shoe o sapato *sa**pah**-too*

shop a loja *lojuh*

shopping: to go shopping ir às compras *eer ash **kom**prush*

short curto(a) *koortoo(uh)*

short-cut o atalho *a**tal**-yoo*

shorts os calções *kal**soynsh***

show[1] *n* o espectáculo *shpe-**ta**kooloo*

show[2] *vb* mostrar *moosh-**trar***

shower o duche *doosh*

shrimps os camarões *kamuh-**roynsh***

sick *(ill)* doente *doo-**ent***

sightseeing a visita a lugares de interesse *vee**zee**tuh uh loogah-rush deentuh-**ress***

sign a tabuleta *taboo-**let**uh*

signature a assinatura *asseenuh-**too**ruh*

silk a seda *say-duh*

silver a prata *prah-tuh*

similar similar *seemee**lar***

simple simples *seemplush*

single *(unmarried)* solteiro(a) *sol**tay**-roo(uh)*; *(not double)* um (uma) único(a) *oom (oomuh) oonikoo(uh)*

single bed a cama de solteiro *kah-muh duh soltay-roo*

single room o quarto individual *kwartoo eendeeveed-wal*

sink o lava-louça *lavuh-loh-suh*

sir senhor *sun-yor*

sister a irmã *eermang*

sit sentar-se *sentar-suh*

size o número *noomeroo*

skate o patim *pateeng*

skating a patinagem *pateenah-jayng*

skimmed milk o leite desnatado *layt duj-natah-doo*

skin a pele *pel*

skin diving a caça submarina *kah-suh soobmuh-reenuh*

skirt a saia *sy-uh*

sleep dormir *doormeer*

sleeper *(in train)* a carruagem-cama *kar-wah-jayng-kahmuh*

sleeping bag o saco cama *sah-koo kahmuh*

sleeping car a carruagem-cama *kar-wah-jayng-kahmuh*

sleeping pill o comprimido para dormir *kompree-meedoo paruh doormeer*

slice a fatia *fatee-uh*

slide *(photograph)* o slide *shlyd*

slippers os chinelos *sheeneloosh*

slow lento(a) *lentoo(uh)*

small pequeno(a) *puh-kaynoo(uh)*

smaller mais pequeno(a) *mysh puh-kay-noo(uh)*

smell *(pleasant)* o cheiro *shay-roo;* *(unpleasant)* o mau cheiro *mow shay-roo*

smoke[1] *n* o fumo *foomoo*

smoke[2] *vb* fumar *foomar*

smoked fumado(a) *foomah-doo(uh)*

snack bar o snack-bar *snack-bar*

snorkel o tubo de ar *tooboo dee ar*

snow a neve *nev*

snowed up cheio(a) de neve *shayoo(uh) duh nev*

snowing: it's snowing está a nevar *shta uh nuh-var*

so: so much tanto(a) *tantoo(uh)*

soap o sabão *sabowng*

soap powder o sabão em pó *sabowng ayng po*

sober sóbrio(a) *sob-ree-oo(uh)*

socket a tomada *toomah-duh*

sock a meia *mayuh*

soda a água bicarbonatada *ahg-wuh beekarboo-natah-duh*

soft macio(a) *masee-oo(uh)*

soft drink a bebida não alcoólica *buh-beeduh nowng alk-wolikuh*

some alguns (algumas) *algoonsh (algoomush)*

someone alguém *algayng*

something alguma coisa *algoomuh koy-zuh*

sometimes às vezes *ash vay-zush*

son o filho *feel-yoo*

song a canção *kansowng*

soon em breve *ayng brev*

sore doloroso(a) *dooloo-roh-zoo(uh)*

sorry: I'm sorry! lamento *lamentoo*

sort: what sort of cheese? que tipo de queijo? *kee teepoo duh kay-joo*

soup a sopa *sopuh*

south o sul *sool*

souvenir a recordação *ruh-koorduh-sowng*

space: parking space o lugar *loogar*

spade a enxada *ayn-shah-duh*

Spain a Espanha *shpan-yuh*

Spanish espanhol(a) *shpan-yol(uh)*

spanner a chave inglesa *shahv eenglay-zuh*

spare wheel a roda sobressalente *roduh sobruh-salent*

sparkling espumoso(a) *shpoomoh-zoo(uh)*

spark plug a vela *veluh*

speak falar *falar*

special especial *shpuss-yal*

speciality a especialidade *shpuss-yalee-dahd*

speed a velocidade *vuh-loossee-dahd*

speed limit o limite de velocidade *leemeet duh vuh-loossee-dahd*

spell: how do you spell it? como se escreve? *koh-moo suh shkrev*

spicy picante *peekant*

spinach o espinafre *shpee-nafruh*

spirits a bebida alcoólica *buh-beeduh alk-wolikuh*

sponge a esponja *shpon-juh*

spoon a colher *kool-yehr*

sport o desporto *dush-portoo*

spring *(season)* a primavera *preemuh-vehruh*

square *(in town)* a praça *prah-suh*

squash *(game)* o squash *squash*; *(drink)* o sumo *soomoo*

stairs a escada *shkah-duh*

stalls *(theatre)* a plateia *platay-uh*

stamp o selo *say-loo*

start começar *koomuh-sar*

starter *(in meal)* a entrada *ayntrah-duh*; *(in car)* o motor de arranque *mootor dee arank*

station a estação *shtasowng*

stationer's a papelaria *papuh-luh-ree-uh*

stay *(remain)* ficar *feekar*; **I'm staying at a hotel** fico num hotel *feekoo noom oh-tel*

steak o bife *beef*

steep íngreme *eengrem*

sterling esterlino(a) *shterleenoo(uh)*

stew o guisado *gheezah-doo*

steward o comissário de bordo *koomee-sar-yoo duh bordoo*

stewardess a hospedeira de bordo *oshpuh-day-ruh duh bordoo*

sticking plaster o penso *pensoo*

still *(motionless)* imóvel *eemovel*

sting a picada *peekah-duh*

stockings as meias de senhora *mayush duh sun-yoruh*

stomach o estômago *shtoh-magoo*

stomach upset o mal-estar de estômago *mal-shtar duh shtoh-magoo*

stop parar *parar*

stopover a interrupção de viagem *eenter-roopsowng duh vee-ah-jayng*

storm a tempestade *tempush-tahd*

straight on sempre em frente *sempruh ayng frent*

straw *(for drinking)* a palha *pal-yuh*

strawberry o morango *moorangoo*

street a rua *roo-uh*

street map o mapa das ruas *mah-puh dush roo-ush*

string o cordel *koordel*

striped às riscas *ash reesh-kush*

strong forte *fort*

stuck bloqueado(a) *blook-yah-doo(uh)*

student o/a estudante *shtoodant*

stung picado(a) *peekah-doo(uh)*

stupid estúpido(a) *shtoopidoo(uh)*

suddenly de repente *duh ruh-pent*

suede a camurça *kamoor-suh*

sugar o açúcar *asookar*

suit o fato *fah-too*

suitcase a mala *mah-luh*

summer o verão *vuh-rowng*

sun o sol *sol*

sunbathe tomar banhos de sol *toomar bahn-yoosh duh sol*

sunburn a queimadura de sol *kaymyh-dooruh duh sol*

sunglasses os óculos de sol *okooloosh duh sol*

sunny soalheiro(a) *swal-yay-roo(uh)*

sunshade o guarda-sol *gwarduh-sol*

sunstroke a insolação *eensooluh-sowng*

suntan lotion a loção de bronzear *loosowng duh bronzee-ar*

supermarket o supermercado *sooper-merkah-doo*

supper *(dinner)* a ceia *sayuh*

supplement o suplemento *soopluh-mentoo*

sure seguro(a) *suh-gooroo(uh)*

surface: by surface mail por superfície *poor sooper-feesee*

surfboard a prancha de surf *pranshuh duh surf*

surfing o surf *soorf*

surname o apelido *apuh-leedoo*

suspension a suspensão *sooshpensowng*

sweater o pulover *pooloh-vehr*

sweet doce *dohss*

sweetener o edulcorante *eedoolkoorant*

sweets os rebuçados *reboosahdoosh*

swim nadar *nadar*

swimming pool a piscina *peeshseenuh*

swimsuit o fato de banho *fah-too duh bahn-yoo*

Swiss suíço(a) *sweesoo(uh)*

switch o interruptor *eenteroop-tor*

switch off apagar *apuh-gar*

switch on acender *asayn-dehr*

Switzerland a Suíça *sweessuh*

synagogue a sinagoga *seenuh-goguh*

table a mesa *may-zuh*

tablecloth a toalha de mesa *twal-yuh duh may-zuh*

tablespoon a colher de sopa *koolyehr duh sopuh*

tablet o comprimido *kompree-meedoo*

table tennis o ténis de mesa *tayneesh duh may-zuh*

take *(carry)* levar *luhvar*; *(grab, seize)* tomar *toomar*

talc o talco *talkoo*

talk conversar *komversar*

tall alto(a) *altoo(uh)*

tampons os tampões *tampoynsh*

tap a torneira *toornay-ruh*

tape a fita *feetuh*

tape recorder o gravador *gravuh-dor*

tartar sauce o molho tártaro *mohl-yoo tartaroo*

taste¹ *vb* : can I taste some? posso provar? *possoo proovar*

taste² *n* o sabor *sabor*

tax o imposto *eemposhtoo*

taxi o táxi *taxee*

taxi rank a praça de táxis *prah-suh duh taxeesh*

tea o chá *sha*

tea bag o saquinho de chá *sakeen-yoo duh sha*

teach ensinar *aynseenar*

teacher o/a profesor(a) *proofuh-sor(uh)*

teapot o bule *bool*

teaspoon a colher de chá *kool-yehr duh sha*

teat a tetina *tuh-teenuh*

teeshirt a T-shirt *tee-shirt*

teeth os dentes *dentsh*

telegram o telegrama *tuh-luh-grah-muh*

telephone o telefone *tuh-luh-fon*

telephone box a cabine telefónica *kabeen tuh-luh-fonikuh*

telephone call a chamada *shamah-duh*

telephone directory a lista telefónica *leeshtuh tuh-luh-fonikuh*

television a televisão *tuh-luh-veezowng*

television set o televisor *tuh-luh-veezor*

telex o telex *telex*

tell dizer a *deezehr uh*

temperature a temperatura *temperuh-tooruh*; **to have a temperature** ter febre *tehr februh*

temporary temporário(a) *tempoo-rar-yoo(uh)*

tennis o ténis *tay-neesh*

tennis court o campo de ténis *kampoo duh tay-neesh*

tennis racket a raqueta de ténis *raketuh duh tay-neesh*

tent a tenda *tenduh*

tent peg a estaca *shtah-kuh*

terminus a estação final *shtasowng feenal*

terrace a esplanada *shplanah-duh*

than: better than melhor do que *mul-yor doo kuh*

thank you obrigado *oh-breegah-doo*; **thank you very much** muito obrigado *mweent oh-breegah-doo*

that aquele (aquela) *akayl (akeluh)*; **that one** esse *ehss*

thaw: it's thawing está a derreter *shta uh duh-ruh-tehr*

theatre o teatro *tee-ah-troo*

then então *entowng*

there ali *alee*; **there is/there are** há *a*

thermometer o termómetro *ter-mometroo*

these estes (estas) *aysh-tush (esh-tush)*

they eles (elas) *aylush (elush)*; *see* **GRAMMAR**

thief o ladrão *ladrowng*

thing a coisa *koy-zuh*; **my things** as minhas coisas *ush meen-yush koy-zush*

think pensar *paynsar*

third terceiro(a) *tersay-roo(uh)*

thirsty: I'm thirsty tenho sede *ten-yoo sed*

this este (esta) *aysht (eshtuh)*; **this one** este *aysht*

those aqueles (aquelas) *akay-lush (akelush)*

thread a linha *leen-yuh*

throat a garganta *gargantuh*

throat lozenges as pastilhas para a garganta *pash-teel-yush pra gargantuh*

through através de *atruh-vesh duh*

thunder o trovão *troovowng*

ticket o bilhete *beel-yet*

ticket collector o revisor *ruh-veezor*

ticket office a bilheteira *beel-yuh-tay-ruh*

tide a maré *mare*

tie a gravata *gruh-vah-tuh*

tights os collants *kolansh*

till[1] *n* a caixa *ky-shuh*

till[2] *conj (until)* até *ate*

time a hora *oruh*; **this time** esta vez *eshtuh vesh*

timetable board o horário *oh-rar-yoo*

tin a lata *lah-tuh*

tinfoil a folha de estanho *fol-yuh dush-tahn-yoo*

tin-opener o abre-latas *ah-bruh-lah-tush*

tip *(to waiter, etc)* a gorjeta *goor-jetuh*

tipped com filtro *kong feeltroo*

tired cansado(a) *kansah-doo(uh)*

tissue o lenço de papel *lensoo duh papel*

to a *uh*; **to London** para Londres *paruh londrush*; **to Spain** para Espanha *paruh shpahn-yuh*

toast a torrada *toorah-duh*

tobacco o tabaco *tabah-koo*

tobacconist's a tabacaria *tabuh-karee-uh*

today hoje *ohj*

together juntos *joontoosh*

toilet a casa de banho *kah-zuh duh bahn-yoo*

toilet paper o papel higiénico *papel eej-yenikoo*

toll a portagem *poortah-jayng*

tomato o tomate *toomat*

tomato juice o sumo de tomate *soomoo duh toomat*

tomorrow amanhã *aman-yang*

tongue a língua *leeng-wuh*

tonic water a água tónica *ahg-wuh tonikuh*

tonight esta noite *eshtuh noyt*

too *(also)* também *tambayng*; *(too much)* demais *duh-mysh*

tooth o dente *dent*

toothache: I have toothache tenho a dor de dentes *taynyoo uh dor duh dentsh*

toothbrush a escova de dentes *shkovuh duh dentsh*

toothpaste a pasta dentífrica *pashtuh dentee-frikuh*

top[1] *adj* : **the top floor** o último andar *ooltimoo andar*

top[2] *n* a parte de cima *part duh seemuh*; **on top of …** em cima de … *ayng seemuh duh …*

torch a lâmpada eléctrica *lahm-paduh eele-trikuh*

torn rasgado(a) *raj-**gah**-doo(uh)*
total o total *too**tal***
tough *(meat)* duro(a) *doo**roo**(uh)*
tour a excursão *shkoor-**sowng***
tourist o turista *too**reesh**-tuh*
tourist office o turismo *too**reej**-moo*
tourist ticket o bilhete turístico
  *beel-**yet** too**reesh**-tikoo*
tow rebocar *ruh-boo**kar***
towel o toalha *t**wal**-yuh*
town a cidade *see**dahd***
town centre o centro da cidade
  sen**troo duh see**dahd
town plan o mapa da cidade *mah-*
  *puh duh see**dahd***
towrope o cabo de reboque *kah-*
  *boo duh ruh-**bok***
toy o brinquedo *breen**kay**-doo*
traditional tradicional *tradeess-*
  *yoo**nal***
traffic o trânsito *tran**zi**too*
trailer o atrelado *atruh-**lah**-doo*
train o comboio *kom**boy**oo*
tram o eléctrico *ee**let**rikoo*
translate traduzir *tradoo**zeer***
translation a tradução *tradoo-**sowng***
travel viajar *vee-uh-**jar***
travel agent o agente de viagens
  *a**jent** duh vee-**ah**-jaynsh*
traveller's cheques o cheque de
  viagem *shek duh vee-**ah**-jayng*
tray o tabuleiro *taboo-**lay**-roo*
tree a árvore *ar**vooruh***
trim aparar *apa**rar***
trip a viagem *vee-**ah**-jayng*
trouble os problemas *proo-**blem**ush*
trousers as calças *kal**sush***

true verdadeiro(a) *verduh-**day**-*
  roo(uh)
trunk *(luggage)* a mala *mah-luh*
trunks os calções de banho
  *kal**soynsh** duh **bahn**-yoo*
try tentar *ten**tar***
try on provar *proo**var***
T-shirt a T-shirt *tee-shirt*
tuna o atum *a**toong***
tunnel o túnel *too**nel***
turkey o peru *puh-**roo***
turn *(handle, wheel)* voltar *vol**tar***
turnip o nabo *nah-boo*
turn off *(light, etc)* apagar *apuh-**gar**;*
  (tap) fechar *fu**shar***
turn on *(light, etc)* acender
  *assen**dehr**; (tap)* abrir *a**breer***
tweezers a pinça *peen**suh***
twice duas vezes *doo-ush **vay**-zush*
twin-bedded room o quarto com
  duas camas *k**war**too kong **doo**-ush
  kah-mush*
typical típico(a) *tee**pikoo**(uh)*
tyre o pneu *p**nay**-oo*
tyre pressure a pressão dos pneus
  *pre**sowng** doos **pnay**-oosh*

umbrella o guarda-chuva *gwarduh-*
  *shoo**vuh***
uncomfortable incómodo(a) *een-*
  ***kom**oodoo(uh)*
unconscious inconsciente *een-*
  *konsh-see-**ent***
under debaixo de *duh-**by**-shoo duh*
underground o metropolitano
  *metroo-poolee-**tah**-noo*
underpass a passagem subterrânea
  *pa**sah**-jayng soobte**rah**-nee-uh*

understand compreender *kompree-endehr*; **I don't understand** não compreendo *nowng kompree-endoo*

underwear a roupa interior *roh-puh eenteree-or*

United States os Estados Unidos *shtah-dooz oonee-doosh*

university a universidade *oonee-versee-dahd*

unpack *(case)* desfazer *dush-fazehr*

up levantado(a) *luh-vantah-doo(uh)*; **up there** lá em cima *la ayng seemuh*

upstairs lá em cima *la ayng seemuh*

urgent urgente *oorjent*

use utilizar *ooteelee-zar*

useful útil *ooteel*

usual habitual *abeet-wal*

usually geralmente *juh-ralment*

vacancies *(rooms)* os quartos vagos *kwartoosh vah-goosh*

vacuum cleaner o aspirador *ash-peeruh-dor*

valid válido(a) *validoo(uh)*

valley o vale *val*

valuable valioso(a) *val-yoh-zoo(uh)*

valuables os objectos de valor *objetoosh duh valor*

van a carrinha *kareen-yuh*

vase o vaso *vah-zoo*

VAT o IVA *eevuh*

veal a carne de vitela *karn duh veeteluh*

vegetables os legumes *luh-goomush*

vegetarian vegetariano(a) *vejuh-tuh-ree-ah-noo(uh)*

ventilator o ventilador *venteeluh-dor*

vermouth o vermute *vermoot*

very muito *mweentoo*

vest a camisola interior *kamee-zoluh eenteree-or*

via via *vee-uh*

view a vista *veeshtuh*

villa a casa de campo *kah-zuh duh kampoo*

village a aldeia *aldayuh*

vinegar o vinagre *veenah-gruh*

vineyard a vinha *veen-yuh*

visa o visto *veeshtoo*

visit visitar *veezeetar*

vitamin a vitamina *veetuh-meenuh*

vodka o vodka *vodkuh*

voltage a voltagem *voltah-jayng*

waist a cintura *seen-tooruh*

wait (for) esperar (por) *shpuh-rar (poor)*

waiter o empregado de mesa *aympruh-gah-doo duh may-zuh*

waiting room a sala de espera *sah-luh dush-pehruh*

waitress a empregada de mesa *aympruh-gah-duh duh may-zuh*

wake up acordar *akoordar*

Wales o País de Gales *pa-eesh duh gah-lush*

walk[1] *vb* andar *andar*

walk[2] *n* o passeio *pasayoo*

wallet a carteira *kartay-ruh*

walnut a noz *nosh*

want querer *kuh-rehr*

warm quente *kent*

warning triangle o triângulo *tree-angooloo*

wash lavar *lavar*; **to wash oneself**

lavar-se *lavar-suh*

washbasin o lavatório *lavuh-***tor**-*yoo*

washing machine a máquina de lavar roupa **mak***inuh duh la***var** roh*-puh*

washing powder o detergente para a roupa *duh-ter***jent** *pra* **roh**-*puh*

washing-up liquid o detergente para a louça *duh-ter***jent** *pra* **loh**-*suh*

wasp a vespa **vesh***puh*

waste bin o caixote do lixo *ky-***shot** *doo* **lee***shoo*

watch[1] *n* o relógio *ruh-***loj**-*yoo*

watch[2] *vb (look at)* ver *vehr*

water a água **ahg**-*wuh*

waterfall a queda de água **ked***uh* **dahg**-*wuh*

water heater o esquentador *shkentuh-***dor**

watermelon a melancia *melan-***see**-*uh*

waterproof impermeável *eempermee-***ah**-*vel*

water-skiing o esqui aquático *shkee akwatikoo*

wave *(on sea)* a onda *on***duh**

wax a cera **seh***ruh*

way *(manner)* a maneira *ma***nay**-*ruh*; *(route)* o caminho *ka***meen**-*yoo*; **this way** por aqui *poor a***kee**

we nós *nosh*; *see* GRAMMAR

weak *(person)* fraco(a) *frah-***koo**(*uh*); *(coffee)* aguado(a) *ag***wah**-*doo*

wear vestir *vush-***teer**

weather o tempo **tem***poo*

wedding o casamento *kazuh-***men***too*

week a semana *se***mah**-*nuh*

weekday o dia útil **dee**-*uh* **oo***teel*

weekend o fim de semana *feeng duh se***mah**-*nuh*

weekly *(rate, etc)* por semana *poor se***mah**-*nuh*

weight o peso **pay**-*zoo*

welcome bemvindo(a) *bayng-***veen***doo*(*uh*)

well bem *bayng*; **he's not well** não se sente bem *nowng suh sent bayng*; **well done** *(steak)* bem passado(a) *bayng pa***sah**-*doo*(*uh*)

Welsh galês (galesa) *ga***lesh** (*ga***lay**-*zuh*)

west o oeste *wesht*

wet molhado(a) *mohl-***yah**-*doo*(*uh*)

wetsuit o fato de mergulhador **fah***too duh mergool-yuh-***dor**

what que; **what is it?** o que é? *oo kee e*

wheel a roda **rod***uh*

wheelchair a cadeira de rodas *ka***day**-*ruh duh* **rod***ush*

when quando **kwan***doo*

where onde **on***duh*

which: which is it? qual é? *kwal e*

while enquanto *ayn-***kwan***too*; **in a while** dentro de pouco **den***troo duh* **poh**-*koo*

whipped batido(a) *ba***tee***doo*(*uh*)

whisky o whisky **weesh***kee*

white branco(a) **brank***oo*(*uh*)

who: who is it? quem é? *kayng e*

whole inteiro(a) *een***tay**-*roo*(*uh*)

wholemeal integral *eentuh-***gral**

whose: whose is it? de quem é? *duh* **kayng** *e*

why porquê? *poor***kay**

wide largo(a) **lar***goo*(*uh*)

wife a mulher *mool-***yehr**

window a janela *janeluh; (shop)* a montra *montruh*

windscreen o pára-brisas *paruh-breezush*

windsurfing o wind-surf *weend-soorf*

windy: it's windy está vento *shta ventoo*

wine o vinho *veen-yoo*

wine list a lista de vinhos *leesh-tuh duh veen-yoosh*

winter o inverno *eemvehr-noo*

with com *kong*

without sem *sayng*

woman a mulher *mool-yehr*

wood a madeira *maday-ruh; (forest)* a floresta *flooreshtuh*

wool a lã *lang*

word a palavra *palahv-ruh*

work *(person)* trabalhar *trabal-yar; (machine, car)* funcionar *foonss-yoonar*

worried preoccupado(a) *pree-okoo-pah-doo(uh)*

worse pior *pee-or*

worth: it's worth 2000 escudos vale dois mil escudos *vahl doysh meel shkoodoosh*

wrap (up) embrulhar *aym-brool-yar*

wrapping paper o papel de embrulho *papel daym-brool-yoo*

write escrever *shkruh-vehr*

writing paper o papel de carta *papel duh kartuh*

wrong errado(a) *erah-doo(uh);* **sorry, wrong number** enganou-se no número *aynga-noh-suh noo noomero*

yacht o iate

year o ano *ah-noo*

yellow amarelo(a) *amuh-reloo(uh)*

yes sim *seeng;* **yes please** sim, por favor *seeng poor favor*

yesterday ontem *ontayng*

yet: not yet ainda não *uh-eenduh nowng*

yoghurt o iogurte *yoogoort*

you *(formal)* você *voh-se; (with friends)* tu *too; (plural)* vocês *voh-sesh; (with friends)* vos *vosh; see* **GRAMMAR**

young novo(a) *noh-voo(uh)*

youth hostel o albergue da juventude *albehrg duh jooven-tood*

zero o zero *zehroo*

zip o fecho éclair *fay-shoo ay-klehr*

zoo o jardim zoológico *jardeeng zoh-oolojikoo*

a to; the; **a dez quilómetros** ten kilometres away

à to the

abacate *m* avocado

abadia *f* abbey

abaixo down

abastecer to supply

abelha *f* bee

aberto(a) open; **aberto todo o ano** open all year round; **aberto das ... às ... horas** open from ... to ... o'clock

abóbora *f* pumpkin

abóbora-menina *f* marrow *(vegetable)*

abrande slow down

abre-garrafas *m* bottle-opener

abre-latas *m* tin-opener; can-opener

Abril *m* April

abrir to open; to unlock *(door)*

absorventes diários *mpl* mini-pads

acabar to end; to finish

acampar to camp

aceitar to accept

acelerador *m* accelerator

acelerar to accelerate

acender to switch on; to turn on *(radio, etc)*; to light *(fire, cigarette)*; **acenda as luzes** switch on headlights; **acenda os médios** switch on dipped headlights

acepipes *mpl* titbits

aceso(a) on *(light, etc)*

acesso *m* access

acetona *f* nail polish remover

achar to think

acidente *m* accident

acima above

aço *m* steel; **aço inoxidável** stainless steel

acomodações *fpl* accommodation

aconselhável advisable; **não aconselhável a menores de ... anos** not recommended for those under ... years of age

açorda *f* bread soup; **açorda à alentejana** bread and fish soup; **açorda de bacalhau** cod in thick bread soup; **açorda de camarão** shrimps in thick bread and egg soup; **açorda de marisco** thick bread soup with shellfish

Açores *mpl* the Azores; region producing dry, fruity white wines

ACP *see* **automóvel**

actividades *fpl* activities

actual present(-day)

actualizar to modernize

açúcar *m* sugar

adega *f* wine cellar

adesivo *m* plaster *(for cut)*

adeus goodbye

adiamento *m* postponement

adiantado(a) fast *(watch, etc)*

adiar to postpone

admissão *f* admission

admitir to admit

adolescente *m/f* teenager

adquirir to acquire

adulto(a) adult

advogado *m* lawyer

aéreo(a): a linha aérea airline; **via aérea** air mail

aeroporto *m* airport

afastar to keep away
afinar to adjust
afixar to stick
afrouxar to slow down
agência f agency; **agência
imobiliária** estate agent; **agência de
viagens** travel agents
agente m/f agent; **agente de compra
e venda de propriedades** estate
agent
agitar to shake; to stir; **agitar bem
antes de usar** shake well before use
agora now
Agosto m August
agradecer to thank
agradecimento m thanks
agrião m watercress
água f water; **água bicarbonatada**
soda water; **água de colónia** toilet
water; **água corrente quente e fria**
hot and cold running water; **água
destilada** distilled water; **água
mineral** mineral water; **água
potável** drinking water; **água tónica**
tonic water
água-pé f diluted wine
aguardar to wait
aguardente f spirit brandy;
aguardente velha matured grape
brandy
agudo(a) sharp (pain)
aí there
aipo m celery
ajudar to help
alameda f alley
alarme m alarm
albergue m hostel; **albergue da
juventude** youth hostel

alcachofra f artichoke
alcatifa f carpet (fitted)
alcatra f: **alcatra à moda dos Açores**
roast veal in wine sauce
alcoólico(a) alcoholic; **bebida
alcoólica** alcoholic drink
aldeia f village
alegre glad
além over there
Alemanha f Germany
Alentejo region producing full-
bodied red and white wines
alérgico(a) a allergic to
alface f lettuce
alfaiate m tailor
alfândega f customs
alfinete m pin
alforreca f jellyfish
algarismo m number (figure)
algodão m cotton
alguém somebody; anybody (in
questions)
algum(a) some; any; **alguns
(algumas)** a few; some; **mais alguma
coisa?** anything else?
alheira f garlic sausage
alho m garlic
alhos-porros mpl leeks
ali there
alimentação f food
alinhamento m steering;
alinhamento de direcções steering
alignment
alívio m relief
almoço m lunch
almofada f pillow; cushion
almôndegas fpl meatballs

alojamento *m* accommodation

alperche *m* apricot

alpinismo *m* climbing

alterar to change

alternador *m* alternator

alto! stop!

alto(a) high; tall; loud; **a estação alta** high season; **alta costura** haute couture

altura *f* height

alugar to hire; to rent; to let *(rent out)*; **quarto para alugar** vacancy; **aluga-se** for hire; to rent; **alugam-se quartos** rooms to let

aluguer *m* rental; **aluguer de motorizadas** motorbike hire/rental; **aluguer de vivendas e apartamentos mobilados** furnished villas and flats to let

amanhã tomorrow

amarelo(a) yellow

amargo(a) bitter

ambiente *m* atmosphere; **ambiente familiar** friendly atmosphere; **ambiente típico** traditional surroundings

ambulância *f* ambulance

amêijoa *f* clam; cockle; **amêijoas à Bulhão pato** clams with coriander, onion and garlic; **amêijoas na cataplana** layers of pork, clams, ham and onion

ameixa *f* plum; **ameixa seca** prune

amêndoa *f* almond; **amêndoa amarga** bitter almond liqueur

amendoim *m* peanut

amigdalite *f* tonsillitis

amigo(a) *m/f* friend

amora *f* blackberry; mulberry

amortecedor *m* shock absorber

amostra *f* sample

ampliações *mpl* enlargements

analgésico *m* painkiller

ananás *m* pineapple

anchovas *fpl* anchovies

andar[1] to walk

andar[2] *m* floor; storey; **andares de luxo** luxury flats

andebol *m* handball

anel *m* ring

angina *f* sore throat

anis *m* aniseed

aniversário *m* anniversary; birthday

ano *m* year; **Ano Novo** New Year

antena *f* aerial

antes de before

anti-aderente nonstick

antibiótico *m* antibiotic

anticonceptivo *m* contraceptive

antigamente in the past

antigo(a) ancient

antiguidades *fpl* antiques

antitranspirante *m* antiperspirant

apagado(a) off *(radio, etc)*; out *(light, etc)*

apagar to switch off *(light, etc)*; to turn off *(radio, etc)*

aparelhagem de som *f* audio equipment

aparelho *m* gadget; machine; **aparelho para a surdez** hearing aid

apartamento *m* apartment; flat; **apartamento com cozinha** self-catering flat

apelido *m* surname; **apelido de**

solteira maiden name
apenas only
aperitivo *m* aperitif
apertado(a) tight
apertar to fasten; to squeeze; **apertar o cinto de segurança** fasten your seat belt
apetite *m* appetite; **bom apetite!** enjoy your meal!
apólice *f* : **apólice de segura** insurance certificate
apresentar to introduce
aquário *m* aquarium
aquecedor *m* heater; electric fire
aquecimento *m* heating
aquele (aquela) that; **aqueles (aquelas)** those
aqui here
ar *m* air; choke *(car)*; **ar e água** air and water *(at garage)*; **ar condicionado** air conditioning; **o filtro de ar** air filter; **ao ar livre** outdoor; **o tubo de ar** snorkel
árabe Arabian
arder to burn
areia *f* sand
arenque *m* herring
argolas *fpl* doughnut rings
arma *f* : **arma de fogo** gun
armário *m* cupboard; closet
armazém *m* : **grande armazém** department store
arraial *m* open-air festival
arrefecer to cool down *(weather)*; to grow cold *(food)*
arrendar to let
arroz *m* rice; **arroz de atum** rice and tuna in mayonnaise, egg and tomato; **arroz doce** sweet rice dessert; **arroz de frango** chicken rissotto; **arroz de marisco** shrimps and clams with rice; **arroz à valenciana** a type of paella
artesanato *m* handicrafts
artigo *m* item; **artigos fotográficos** photographic equipment; **artigos de menage** household goods; **artigos de praia** beachwear; **artigos regionais** regional handicrafts; **artigos de viagem** travel goods; **artigos de vime** wickerwork
árvore *m* tree
as the
ascensor *m* lift; elevator
aspirar to hoover
assado(a) roast
assalto *m* assault
assim like this
assinar to sign
assinatura *f* signature
assistência *f* audience; assistance
assistir to attend; to assist
atacadores *mpl* laces
até till; until; even
atenção *f* attention; caution; **atenção!** pay attention!; **atenção ao comboio** beware of trains; **atenção porta automática** attention: automatic door; **atenção zona escolar – seja prudente** school ahead – drive carefully
atendimento *m* : **atendimento preferencial** preferential service
Atentamente Yours faithfully
aterrar to land
atletismo *m* athletics
atrás behind

atrasado(a) late *(for appointment)*; **o comboio está atrasado dez minutos** the train is 10 minutes late

atrasar to delay

atravessar to cross; **atravesse pela passadeira** use the zebra crossing

atrelado *m* trailer

atum *m* tuna; tunny fish

autobrilhante *m* polish

autocarro *m* bus; coach; **a paragem de autocarro** bus stop

autoclismo *m* : **o autoclismo não funciona** the toilet won't flush

autocolante self-adhesive

autoestrada *f* motorway; **autoestrada com portagem** toll motorway

automatizada *f* bus using ticket machine

automobilista *m/f* driver

automóvel *m* car; **Automóvel Clube de Portugal (ACP)** Portuguese RAC; **automóveis de aluguer** car hire

autorização *f* licence; permit

avance go ahead

avaria *f* breakdown

avariado(a) broken down; out of order

avarias *fpl* breakdown service

ave *f* bird

aveia *f* oats

avelã *f* hazelnut

avenida *f* avenue

avião *m* plane

aviso *m* warning; **aviso prévio** notice *(time)*

avô *m* grandfather

avó *f* grandmother

azedo(a) bitter

azeite *m* olive oil

azeitona *f* olive

azerias *fpl* potato and almond fritters

azul blue

azulejo *m* ornamental tile

bacalhau *m* cod; **bacalhau à Brás** cod with eggs, onion and potatoes; **bacalhau à Gomes de Sá** cod with onions and potatoes; **bacalhau à lagareiro** mashed potato and oven-roasted cod; **bacalhau à portuguesa** baked cod with potato and onions; **bacalhau com todos** cod with potatoes, onion, vegetables and coriander; **bacalhau à Zé do Pipo** cod in egg sauce

bagaço *m* wine brandy

bagagem *f* luggage; baggage

bailado *m* dance

Bairrada region producing full-bodied red and aromatic white wines

bairro *m* quarter; district

baixar to lower; **baixar os máximos** to dip one's headlights

baixo: em baixo below; **para baixo** down

baixo(a) low; short

balcão *m* balcony; counter *(in bank, shop)*; circle *(in theatre)*; bar

balneário *m* changing room

bancada *f* stall

banco *m* bank; seat *(in car, etc)*

banheiro *m* lifeguard

banhista *m* bather

banho *m* bath; **com banho privativo** with private bathroom; **a casa de banho** bathroom; toilet; **a touca de banho** bathing cap; **tomar banho** to bathe; to take a bath

baptizado *m* christening

barato(a) cheap

barba *f* beard

barco *m* boat; ship; **barco a motor** motor boat; **barco pneumático** rubber dinghy; **barco a remos** rowing boat; **barco à vela** sailing boat; **barcos de aluguer** boats for hire; **barcos para pesca e recreio** fishing and pleasure boats

barraca *f* hut *(shed)*; sunshade

barragem *f* dam; reservoir

barriga *f* stomach

barros *mpl* clay pottery

barulho *m* noise

batata *f* potato; **o puré de batata** mashed potato; **batatas assadas** baked potatoes; **batatas cozidas** boiled potatoes; **batatas fritas** chips; crisps

bate-chapas *m* panel-beater; body repairs

bater: bata à porta please knock

bateria *f* battery *(for car)*

batido de leite *m* milk shake

bâton *m* lipstick; **bâton para o cieiro** lip salve

baunilha *f* vanilla

bebé *m* baby

beber to drink; **não beber** do not drink

bebida *f* drink

beco *m* alley; lane; **beco sem saída** dead end

Beiras area renowned for light, spicy red wines and sharp refreshing white wines

beleza *f* beauty

beliche *m* berth *(bed)*

belo(a) beautiful; **belos panoramas** fabulous views

bem well; **está bem** OK; **muito bem!** fine!; **bem passado** well done *(steak)*

bemvindo(a) welcome

bengaleiro *m* cloakroom

beringela *f* aubergine

berma *f* hard shoulder; **bermas baixas** steep verge – no hard shoulder

besugo *m* sea bream; **besugo na grelha** charcoal-grilled sea bream

beterraba *f* beetroot

biberão *m* feeding bottle

bica *f* small strong black coffee

bicha *f* queue; **fazer bicha** to queue

bicicleta *f* bicycle; cycle

bifanas *fpl* pork fillets in garlic and wine sauce

bife *m* steak; **bife de alcatra** rump steak; **bife com batatas fritas** steak and chips; **bife de carne picada** hamburger; **bife grelhado** grilled steak

bifurcação *f* junction

bilhar *m* billiards

bilhete *m* ticket; fare; **bilhete de entrada** admission charge; **bilhete postal** postcard; **bilhete turístico** tourist ticket; **bilhetes à venda** tickets on sale

bilheteira *f* booking office; ticket office; box office

binóculos *mpl* binoculars
biscoito *m* flat biscuit
bitoque *m* steak, fried eggs and chips
blusa *f* blouse
blusão *m* short jacket
boa *see* **bom**
boca *f* mouth
bocadinho *m* : **um bocadinho** a little bit
boite *f* nightclub
bola *f* ball; **bola de Berlim** doughnut
bolacha *f* thick biscuit
bolinhos *mpl* dainty cakes
bolo *m* small cake; **bolo rei** cake eaten at Christmas
Bolsa *f* stock exchange
bom (boa) good; fine *(weather)*; well; **bom dia** good morning; **boa noite** good evening; good night; **boa tarde** good afternoon
bomba *f* bomb; pump; **bomba de gasolina** petrol pump; petrol station
bombeiros *mpl* fire brigade
bombom *m* chocolate sweet
boneco *m* doll; puppet toy
bonito(a) pretty
borbulha *f* heat rash; spots *(on skin)*
bordados *mpl* embroidered items
borrachinhos *mpl* cakes soaked in liqueur
borrego *m* lamb; **borrego assado no forno** roast lamb; **borrego à jardineira** lamb stew
bosque *m* forest
bota *f* boot *(to wear)*
boutique *f* fashion shop

braçadeiras *fpl* armbands
bracelete *f* strap; bracelet
braço *m* arm
branco(a) white
breve: em breve soon
brigada *f* : **brigada de trânsito** traffic police
brilhante bright; shiny
brincar to play *(children)*
brincos *mpl* earrings
brindes *mpl* presents; gifts
brinquedo *m* toy
brisa *f* breeze
britânico(a) British
broa *f* corn cake
bronzeador *m* suntan oil
brushing *m* blow-dry
Bucelas *m* area near Lisbon known for its dry white wine
bugigangas *fpl* bric-à-brac
buscar: ir buscar to fetch; **mandar buscar** to send for
bússola *f* compass
buzinar: buzine só quando necessário use your horn only when necessary

cá here
cabeça *f* head
cabedais *mpl* leather goods
cabeleireiro *m* hairdresser
cabelo *m* hair; **o corte de cabelo** haircut
cabide *m* coat hanger; hook *(for coats)*; peg *(for clothes)*
cabine *f* : **cabine telefónica** telephone box

cabo *m* handle *(of knife)*; lead *(electric)*; **cabos de emergência** jump leads; **cabo de reboque** tow rope

cabrito *m* kid goat; **cabrito assado** roast kid

caça *f* game *(to eat)*; hunting; **caça submarina** spear fishing

caçar to hunt

caçarola *f* saucepan; casserole dish

cacau *m* cocoa

cachecol *m* scarf *(long)*

cachimbo *m* pipe

cacholeira *f* smoked sausage

cachorro *m* hot dog

cada each; every

cadeado *m* padlock

cadeira *f* chair; **cadeira de bebé** high chair; push chair; **cadeira de lona** deck chair; **cadeira de rodas** wheelchair

caderneta de bilhetes *f* book of tickets

café *m* (black) coffee; café; **café instantâneo** instant coffee; **café com leite** white coffee; **café torrado** roast coffee

cair to fall

cais *m* quay

caixa *f* box *(container)*; cashier; cash desk; till; **caixa automática** cash machine/dispenser; **caixa do correio** letterbox; **caixa fechada** till closed; **caixa de primeiros socorros** first aid box

caixote *m* bin

calçada *f* slope

calçado *m* footwear

calças *fpl* trousers

calções *mpl* shorts; **calções de banho** trunks

calços para travões *mpl* brake pads

caldeirada *f* fish stew

caldo *m* stock *(for soup)*; **caldo verde** cabbage soup

calibragem *f* wheel alignment

calmante *m* tranquillizer

calor *m* heat; **está calor** it's hot *(weather)*

calorífero *m* heater

cama *f* bed; **cama de campismo** camp bed; **cama de casal** double bed; **cama de criança** cot; **a roupa de cama** bedding

câmara *f*: **câmara de ar** inner tube; **câmara municipal** town hall

camarão *m* shrimp; **camarões cozidos** boiled shrimps; **camarões fritos** shrimps fried in garlic and lemon sauce

camarote *m* cabin

cambiar to exchange; to change *(money)*

câmbio *m* exchange rate

camião *m* lorry

caminho *m* track *(path)*; way; path; **qual é o caminho para …?** which is the way to …?; **caminho de ferro** railway; **Caminhos de Ferro Portugueses (CP)** Portuguese Railways

camioneta *f* bus; delivery van

camisa *f* shirt; **camisa de noite** nightdress

camisaria *f* men's shop

camisola *f* jersey; **camisola de gola alta** polo neck; **camisola interior** vest

campaínha *f* bell *(on door)*

campismo *m* camping

campista *m/f* camper

campo *m* field; country *(not town)*; **campo de futebol** football pitch; **campo de golfe** golf course; **campo de tiro** shooting range; **campo de ténis** tennis court

camurça *f* suede

canção *f* song

cancelado(a) cancelled

cancelar to cancel

canela *f* cinnamon

caneta *f* pen

canja *f* chicken soup

cano de esgoto *m* drain

canoagem *f* canoeing

cansado(a) tired

cantina *f* canteen

cão *m* dog; **cão de guarda** guard dog

capa *f* : **capa impermeável de nylon** cagoule

capacete *m* crash helmet

capela *f* chapel

capot *m* bonnet *(of car)*

cara *f* face

caracóis *mpl* snails

caramelos *mpl* sweets

caranguejo *m* crab

carapau *m* mackerel; **carapaus assados** roast mackerel

caravana *f* caravan

carburador *m* carburettor

carga *f* refill; load; **carga máxima** maximum load

caril *m* curry

carimbo *m* rubber stamp

carioca *m* weak coffee; **carioca de limão** lemon tea

carne *f* meat; **carne de borrego** lamb; **carne picada** mince; **carne de porco** pork; **carne de porco à alentejana** pork, cockles and chips; **carne de vaca** beef; **carne de vaca assada** roast beef; **carne de veado** venison; **carne de vitela** veal; **carnes frias** cold meats; **carnes fumadas** smoked meats

carneiro *m* mutton

caro(a) dear; expensive

carregue: carregue no botão press the button

carreiras *fpl* : **carreiras regulares** regular service *(bus, etc)*

carrinha *f* van

carrinho *m* : **carrinho para a bagagem** luggage trolley; **carrinho de bebé** pram; carry cot

carro *m* car; **carros de aluguer** car hire/rental

carruagem *f* carriage *(railway)*; coach *(on train)*; **carruagem-cama** sleeper *(railway)*

carruagem-restaurante *f* restaurant car

carta *f* letter; **carta verde** green card

cartão *m* card; business card; cardboard; **cartão bancário** cheque card; **cartão de crédito** credit card; **cartão de embarque** boarding card; **cartão de felicitações** greetings

card; **cartão garantia** cheque card;
cartão jovem youth pass

cartaz m notice *(poster)*; list of films
now showing

carteira f wallet

carteirista m pickpocket

carteiro m postman

carvão m coal

casa f home; house; **casa de banho**
toilet; bathroom; **casa de fados**
restaurant where 'fados' are sung;
casa de jantar dining room; **casa de
pasto** cheap eating house; **casa de
saúde** nursing home; **casa da sorte**
lottery office; **a dona de casa**
housewife; **o vinho da casa** house
wine

casaco m jacket; coat

casado(a) married

casal m couple

casamento m wedding

caso m : **em caso de acidente marque
115** in case of accident ring 115;
**em caso de dificuldade nas ligações,
marque 099** if you have any
problems with dialling, ring 099;
em caso de emergência in case of
emergency; **em caso de incêndio** in
case of fire

castanha f chestnut; **castanhas
assadas** roast chestnuts; **castanhas
piladas** dried chestnuts

castanho(a) brown

castelo m castle

catedral f cathedral

católico(a) Catholic

cautela take care

cavala f mackerel

cavaleiro m horseman; rider

cavalheiro m gentleman;
cavalheiros Gentlemen; Gents'

cavalo m horse

cave (c/v) f cellar; basement

cebola f onion

cedo early

cego(a) blind

ceia f supper

ceifa f harvest

célebre famous

cemitério m cemetery

cenoura f carrot

centeio m rye

centígrado m centigrade

centímetro m centimetre

cento: por cento per cent

centro m centre; **centro da cidade**
city/town centre; **centro comercial**
shopping centre; **centro de
enfermagem** clinic; **centro de saúde**
health centre

cera f wax

cerâmica f pottery

cerca: cerca de 50 about 50

cérebro m brain

cereja f cherry

certeza f : **ter a certeza** to be sure;
com certeza of course

certificado m certificate

certo(a) right *(correct, accurate)*;
certain

cerveja f beer; lager; **cerveja preta**
bitter *(beer)*

cervejaria f pub

cesto m basket

céu m sky

cevada f barley

chá f tea; **chá de limão** lemon tea; **chá de tília** linden blossom tea

chamada f telephone call; **chamada gratuita** free call; **chamada internacional** international call; **chamada interurbana** long distance call; **chamada local** local call; **chamada pagável no destino** reverse charge call

chamar to call

chamar-se to be called; **chamo-me ...** my name is ...

champanhe m champagne

champô m shampoo

chanfana f lamb casserole; **chanfana à Bairrada** veal in red wine

chão m floor

chapa f : **chapa de matrícula** number plate

chapéu m hat; **chapéu de sol** sunhat

charcada f caramel and egg yolk dessert

charcutaria f delicatessen

charuto m cigar

chave f key

chávena f cup

check-in m : **fazer o check-in** to check in

chefe m boss; **chefe de cozinha** chef; **chefe de estação** station master

chegadas fpl arrivals

chegar to arrive

cheio(a) full; **o hotel está cheio** the hotel is fully booked

cheirar to smell

cheque m cheque; **cheque de viagem** traveller's cheque; **levantar um cheque** to cash a cheque

cherne m black jewfish

chifre m horn

chispe no forno m roast pig's trotters

chocar contra to crash into

chocos mpl cuttlefish; **chocos com tinta** cuttlefish cooked in their ink

chouriço m spicy sausage

churrascaria f barbecue restaurant

churrasco m barbecue; **no churrasco** barbecued

chuva f rain

chuveiro m shower

Cia. see **companhia**

ciclomotor m motorbike

cidadão (cidadã) m/f citizen

cidade f town; city; **o centro da cidade** town centre; **o mapa de cidade** town plan

cidra f cider

cigarro m cigarette

cima f : **em cima de** on (top of); **para cima** upwards

cimbalino m small strong black coffee

cinco five

cine-teatro m cinema theatre

cinta f corset

cinto m belt; **cinto de salvação** lifebelt; **cinto de segurança** seat belt

cintura f waist

cinzeiro m ashtray

cinzento(a) grey

circo m circus

circuito m : **circuito turístico** round

trip; **com circuitos fechados de televisão** with closed-circuit television

circular *f* roundabout *(for traffic)*

circule: circule pela direita/esquerda keep right/left; **circule com velocidade reduzida** slow; drive slowly

cirurgia *f* surgery

claro(a) light *(colour)*; clear *(transparent)*; bright *(room, weather)*

classe *f* class; **de 2a classe** second class

cliente *m/f* client

clima *m* climate

clínica *f* clinic; **clínica dentária** dental clinic; **clínica geral** general practitioner's

clube *m* club

cobertor *m* blanket

cobrador *m* conductor *(in bus)*

cobrança *f*: **cobrança pelo guarda-freio** pay the brakeman *(on tram)*; **cobrança pelo motorista** pay the driver

cobre *m* copper

cobrir to cover

coco *m* coconut

código *m* code; dialling code; **código postal** postcode

codorniz *f* quail; **codornizes fritas** fried quail

coelho *m* rabbit; **coelho de fricassé** rabbit fricassee

coentro *m* coriander

cofre *m* safe

cofre-nocturno *m* night safe

cogumelo *m* mushroom

coisa *f* thing

cola *f* glue

colar¹ *n* necklace

colar² *vb* to stick

Colares area on the coast near Lisbon renowned for its sharp red wines and fruity whites

colcha *f* bedspread

colchão *m* mattress; **colchão de molas** spring mattress; **colchão pneumático** air mattress; rubber dinghy

colecção *f* collection *(of stamps etc)*

colégio *m* school

colete *m* waistcoat; **colete de salvação** life jacket

colher *f* spoon

cólica *f* colic

colina *f* hill

collants *mpl* tights

colocar to place

colorau *m* paprika

coluna *f* pillar; **coluna vertebral** spine

com with

comandos *mpl* controls

combinação *f* petticoat

comboio *m* train; **comboio directo** direct train; **comboio rápido** express train

combustível *m* fuel

começar to begin; to start

comer to eat

comércio *m* trade; business

comichão *f* itch

comida *f* food

comissário de bordo *m* steward;

purser

como as; how; **como disse?** I beg your pardon?; **como está?** how are you?

comodidade f convenience; **para comodidade do público os lugares são marcados** all seats are numbered for the convenience of the public

companhia (Cia.) f company; **companhias de aviação** airline companies

compartimento m compartment

competição f competition

completar to complete

completo(a) full; no vacancies

compota f jam

compra f purchase

comprar to buy

compras fpl shopping; **ir às compras** to go shopping

compreender to understand

comprido(a) long

comprimento m length

comprimido m pill; tablet

concelho m council

concentrado de tomate m tomato purée

concerto m concert

concordar to agree

concorrente m/f candidate

concurso m : **concurso hípico** horse race

condução f driving; **a carta de condução** driving licence

condutor m driver; chauffeur; **com/sem condutor** with driver/self-drive

conduza: conduza com cuidado drive carefully; **conduza pela direita/esquerda** drive on the right/left

conduzir to drive

confecções fpl : **confecções para senhora** ladies' wear

conferência f conference

conferir to check

confirmar to confirm

confortável comfortable

congelado(a) frozen (food)

congelar to freeze; **não congelar** do not freeze

conhaque m cognac

conhecer to know (person, place)

conjunto m set (of objects); group (musical)

conselho m advice

consertar to repair

consertos mpl repairs

conserva f tinned food

conservar to preserve; **conservar no frio** store in a cold place; **conservar este bilhete até ao fim da viagem** keep your ticket until you arrive

constipação f cold

consulado m consulate

consulta f consultation; appointment (at dentist, etc)

consultório m surgery; **consultório dentário** dental surgery

consumir: consumir dentro de ... best before ...

conta f account; bill

contactar to contact

contador m meter

contente pleased

conter to contain; **não contem ...** does not contain ...

continuar to go on

conto *m* = 1000 escudos

contra against

contrário *m* opposite

contrato *m* contract

controlo *m* control; **controlo de passaportes** passport control

conversar to talk

convés *m* deck

convidado(a) *m/f* guest

convidar to invite; to ask *(invite)*

convite *m* invitation

copo *m* glass *(container)*

cor *f* colour

coração *m* heart; **coração de vitela recheado** stuffed veal's heart

cordeiro *m* lamb

cor de laranja orange *(colour)*

cor-de-rosa pink

corpo *m* body

correctamente properly

correia *f* strap; **correia de ventoinha** fan belt

correio *m* : **o marco do correio** postbox

correios *mpl* post office; **correios e telecomunicações (CTT)** post office

corrente *f* chain; current; **corrente alterna** alternating current (AC); **corrente contínua** direct current (DC)

correr to flow; to run *(person)*

corrida *f* bullfight; **corridas de cavalos** races

corrimão *m* handrail

cortar to cut; to cut off; **cortar e fazer brushing** cut and blow-dry

corte *m* cut

cortejo *m* procession

cortiça *f* cork

cortina *f* curtain

cortinados *mpl* curtains

coscorões *mpl* orange fritters

costa *f* shore; coast

costela *f* rib

costeleta *f* chop *(meat)*; cutlet

cotonetes *mpl* cotton swabs

cotovelo *m* elbow

couro *m* leather

court *m* court; **court de squash** squash court; **court de ténis de piso rápido** hard court *(tennis)*

couve *f* cabbage; **couves de Bruxelas** Brussels sprouts

couve-flor *f* cauliflower

coxia *f* aisle

cozer to boil

cozido(a) boiled; **mal cozido** underdone; **cozido à portuguesa** beef stew, with beans, vegetables, and spicy sausages

cozinha *f* kitchen

cozinhar to cook

cozinheiro(a) *m/f* cook

CP *see* **caminho**

cravinhos *mpl* cloves

cravo *m* carnation

crédito *m* credit

creme *f* cream; foundation cream; **creme amaciador** conditioner; **creme de barbear** shaving cream; **creme para bronzear** suntan cream;

creme hidratante moisturizer; **creme de limpeza** cleansing cream; **creme de marisco** cream of shellfish soup; **cremes e pomadas** creams and ointments

criança f child; **crianças** children crossing; **crianças até ... anos 10% de desconto** discount of 10% for children under ...

cristal m crystal

cristão (cristã) Christian

croquete m croquette

cru(a) raw

cruz f cross; **a Cruz Vermelha** the Red Cross

cruzamento m junction (crossroads)

cruzeiro m cruise

CTT see **correios**

cuecas fpl briefs; pants

cuidado m care (caution); **tenha cuidado** be careful; **tome cuidado** take care; **cuidado com o cão** beware of the dog

culpa f: **a culpa não foi minha** it was not my fault

cumprimento m greeting

cupão m reply coupon

cúpula f dome

curso m course; **cursos de língua portuguesa** Portuguese language courses

curto(a) short

curva f bend; turning; curve; **curva perigosa** dangerous bend

custar to cost

custo m charge; cost; **ao preço de custo** at cost price

c/v see **cave**

damas fpl Ladies'; draughts (game)

damasco m apricot

dança f dance; **danças folclóricas** folk dancing

dano m damage

Dão fruity red and white wines from the north of Portugal

dar to give; **dar prioridade** to give way

data f date; **data de nascimento** date of birth

de of; from; **de luxo** de luxe

dê: dê prioridade give way

debaixo de under

decidir to decide

décimo(a) tenth

declarar to declare

declive m slope

decote m : **decote em V** V-neck

decreto m decree; law

dedo m finger; **dedo do pé** toe

defeito m flaw

deficiente disabled; handicapped

degelo m thaw

degrau m step (stair)

deitar to throw; **deite o lixo no lixo** put your rubbish in the bin

deitar-se to lie down

deixar to let (allow)

delito m crime

demais too much; too many

demasia f change (money)

demasiado too much; too many

demora f delay

demorado(a) late

demorar to delay

dente m tooth; **dentes** teeth; **dentes postiços** false teeth

dentista m dentist

dentro: dentro de in

dependência f branch (of company, etc)

depilações mpl : **depilações a cera** wax hair removal; waxing

depois after(wards)

depositar to deposit; **deposite moedas na ranhura** place coins in the slot

depósito m deposit (in bank); **depósito de bagagens** left-luggage (office); **o depósito da gasolina** petrol tank

depressa quickly

derrapar to skid

derreter: está a derreter it's thawing

desabitado(a) uninhabited

desafio m match; game (sport)

desaparecido(a) missing

desapertar to loosen

descafeinado m decaffeinated coffee

descansar to rest

descarregar to unload

descartável throw-away; disposable

descascar to peel

descer to go down

descida perigosa f steep hill

descoberta f discovery

descongelar to defrost (food); to de-ice (windscreen)

desconhecido m stranger

descontar to discount

desconto m discount; reduction

descrever to describe

descuidado(a) careless

desculpar to excuse

desculpe excuse me; sorry (apology); **desculpe?** pardon?

desde since

desejar to desire; to wish

desembarcar to disembark

desempregado(a) unemployed

desenho m design (pattern, decoration); drawing

desenvolvido(a) developed

desinchar to go down (swelling)

desinfectante m disinfectant

desinfectar to disinfect

desligado(a) off (engine, gas)

desligar to hang up (phone); to switch off (engine); to turn off (radio); **desligue o motor** switch off your motor; **não desligue** do not hang up (phone)

desmaiar to faint

desodorizante m deodorant; **desodorizante de ambiente** air freshener

despachante m shipper; transport agent

despedir-se to say goodbye

despejar to empty (bottle, etc)

despertador m alarm clock

despesa f expense

despir to undress

desportivo(a) sports; sporty

desporto m sport; **desportos náuticos** sailing; watersports

destilar to distil

destinatário *m* addressee

destino *m* destiny; destination

desvio *m* bypass; detour; diversion; **desvio para estacionamento** lay-by

detergente *m* detergent; **detergente líquido** liquid detergent; washing-up liquid; **detergente para a louça** washing-up liquid; **detergente para a roupa** washing powder

devagar slow down *(on road sign)*; drive slowly

dever: eu devo I must; **deve-me ...** you owe me ...

devolver to give back; to return *(give back)*

dez ten

Dezembro *m* December

dia *m* day; **um dia** one day; **dia útil** weekday; **dias de semana** weekdays

diabético(a) diabetic

diante de before *(place)*

diária *f* daily cost

diariamente daily

diário(a) *m* daily

diarreia *f* diarrhoea

dieta *f* diet

diferença *f* difference

diferente different

difícil difficult

dificuldade *f* difficulty

digestão *f* digestion

diluir: diluir num pouco de água dissolve in a little water

diminuir to reduce

dínamo *m* dynamo

dinheiro *m* money; cash

dique *m* dam

direcção *f* steering; **a coluna da direcção** steering column

directo(a) direct

director *m* director

direita *f* right(-hand side); **à direita** on the right; **para a direita** to the right

direito(a) straight; right(-hand); **Dto.** on the right-hand side *(in addresses)*

direitos *mpl* duty *(tax)*; rights; **isento de direitos** duty-free

disco *m* record *(music, etc)*; **o disco de estacionamento** parking disc

discoteca *f* disco; record shop

discussão *f* discussion; argument

disfarce *m* fancy dress

disponível available

dissolver to dissolve

distância *f* distance

distribuidor *m* distributor

distrito *m* district

divã-cama *f* bed-settee

diversões *fpl* entertainment

divertimento *m* : **divertimentos** entertainment

divertir-se to enjoy oneself; to have fun

dívida *f* debt

divisas *fpl* foreign currency

divorciado(a) divorced

dizer to say

dobrada *f* tripe with chickpeas; **dobrada à moda do Porto** tripe and chicken

dobrado(a) bent

dobrar to fold; **ao dobrar a esquina** round the corner

dobro *m* double

doçaria caseira *f* home-made desserts

doce¹ *adj* sweet *(taste)*

doce² *m* dessert; **doce de amêndoa** almond spread; **doce de ovos** custard-like dessert made with eggs and sugar; **doces regionais** regional desserts

documentos *mpl* documents

doença *f* illness

doente ill; sick

doer to ache; to hurt

dois (duas) two

dólar *m* dollar

domicílio *m* residence

domingo *m* Sunday; **domingos e dias feriados** Sundays and holidays

dono(a) *m/f* owner

dor *f* ache; pain

dormida *f*: **dormida e pequeno almoço** bed and breakfast; **dormida, pequeno almoço e banho** bed and breakfast with bath included

dormir to sleep

Douro region producing port wine

doutor *m* doctor

drogaria *f* drugstore; hardware store

Dto. *see* **direito(a)**

duas two

duche *m* shower

duplo(a) double

duração *f* duration

durante during

durar to last

duro(a) hard; stiff; tough *(meat)*

dúzia *f* dozen

e and

é he/she/it is; you are

economizar to save

écran *m* screen

edifício *m* building

edredão *m* duvet; quilt

educado(a) polite

efervescente sparkling

eficaz effective

exio de roda *m* axle

ela she; her; it

elástico *m* rubber band; elastic band

elástico(a) elastic; rubbery

elas they

ele he; him; it

electricidade *f* electricity

electricista *m* electrician

eléctrico *m* tram

electrodomésticos *mpl* household electrical appliances

eles they

elevador *m* lift

em at; in *(with towns, countries)*; into

emagrecer to grow thin

embaixada *f* embassy

embalagem *f*: **embalagem económica** economy pack; **embalagem familiar** family pack

embarcar to board *(ship, plane)*

embarque *m* embarkation; time of sailing

embraiagem *f* clutch

ementa *f* menu

emergência *f* : **é uma emergência** it's an emergency

emitir to issue

empadão *m* : **empadão de bacalhau** cod, potato, onion and egg baked in a mould; **empadão de carne** meat pie; **empadão de peixe** fish pie

empregado(a) *m/f* waiter; maid; waitress; attendant *(at petrol station)*; assistant *(in shop)*; employee *(in office)*

emprego *m* job

empréstimo *m* loan

empurrar to push

empurre push

EN *see* **estrada**

encarnado(a) red

encerrado(a) closed; **encerrado às segundas-feiras** closed on Mondays

encher to fill (up); to pump up *(tyre, etc)*; **encha o depósito** fill it up *(petrol tank)*

enchidos *mpl* processed meats

encolher to shrink

encomenda *f* parcel

encomendar to order

encontrar to meet

encosta *f* hill *(slope)*

endereço *m* address

energia *f* : **o corte de energia** power cut

enevoado(a) hazy; misty

enfermaria *f* ward

enfermeiro(a) *m/f* nurse

enfermo(a) infirm; ill

enfraquecer to weaken

enganar-se to make a mistake

engano *m* mistake

engarrafado(a) jammed; stuck; bottled

engarrafamento *m* hold-up; traffic jam

engolir to swallow; **não engolir** do not swallow

engordar to fatten

engraxar to polish *(shoes)*

enguia *f* eel; **enguias fritas** fried eels

enjoar to be sick

ensinar to teach

ensopado *m* stew; **ensopado de borrego** lamb stew; **ensopado de enguias** eel stew; **ensopado de lulas** fried squid in onion, garlic and herb sauce

entorse *m* sprain

entrada *f* entrance; starter *(in meal)*; hors d'oeuvre; **entrada livre** admission free; **entrada proibida** no entry

entrar to go in; to come in; to get into *(car, etc)*

entre among; between

entrecosto *m* entrecôte; **entrecosto com amêijoas** entrecôte with clams

entrega *f* : **entrega ao domicílio** home delivery service

entregar to deliver

entrevista *f* interview

entroncamento *m* T-junction

enviar to send

enxaqueca *f* migraine

enxugar to dry

época *f* period

equilíbrio *m* balance; **equilíbrio de rodas** wheels balanced

equipamento m equipment
equitação f riding
ermida f hermitage
errado(a) wrong
erro m mistake
erva f grass; herb
ervanário f herbalist
ervilhas fpl peas
esc. see **escudo**
escada f ladder; stairs; **escada rolante** escalator
escala f stopover (in air travel)
escalfado(a) poached
escalope m escalope; **escalope de carneiro** mutton escalope; **escalope panado** breaded escalope; **escalope de porco** pork escalope; **escalopes de vitela ao Madeira** escalopes of veal in Madeira wine
escape m exhaust
esclarecer to explain
esclarecimento m explanation
escocês (escocesa) Scottish
Escócia f Scotland
escola f school; **escola de condução** driving school
escolher to choose
escorregadio(a) slippery
escova f brush; **escova de dentes** toothbrush; **escova de unhas** nailbrush
escrever to write; **escrever à máquina** to type
escrito: por escrito in writing
escritório m office
escudo (esc.) m escudo
escultura f sculpture

escuro(a) dark (colour); **está escuro** it's dark
escuta listen
escutar to listen to
esferográfica f ballpoint pen
esfregão m cleaning pad
esfregona f mop
esgotado(a) sold out (tickets); exhausted (person)
esgoto m drain
esmalte m enamel
espaçoso(a) roomy
espadarte m swordfish; **espadarte fumado** smoked swordfish
espalhar to scatter
Espanha f Spain
espanhol(a) Spanish
espargo m asparagus
esparguete m spaghetti; **esparguete à bolonhesa** Spaghetti Bolognese
esparregado m puréed spinach
especialidade f speciality; **especialidades regionais** regional dishes our speciality
especiarias fpl spices
espectáculo m show (in theatre etc); **espectáculo de variedades** cabaret
espelho m mirror; **espelho retrovisor** driving mirror
esperar to expect; to hope; **esperar por** to wait for
espetada f kebab; **espetadas à Beiroa** kebabs of pork liver, bacon, kidney and peppers; **espetada de leitão** suckling pig kebab; **espetadas de lulas** squid and bacon kebabs; **espetada de rins** kidney kebab; **espetada de vitela** veal

kebab

espeto *m* skewer

espinafre *m* spinach; **espinafres gratinados** spinach au gratin; **espinafres salteados** spinach with butter sauce

esplanada *f* terrace

esposa *f* wife

espumante *m* sparkling wine

espumoso(a) sparkling *(wine)*

Esq. *see* **esquerda**

esquadra *f* police station

esquecer-se de to forget

esquentador *m* water heater

esquerda *f* left(-hand side); **à esquerda** on the left; **para a esquerda** to the left; **Esq.** on the left(-hand) side *(in addresses)*

esqui *m* ski; **esqui aquático** water-skiing

esquiar to ski

esquina *f* corner *(outside)*

estabelecimento *m* shop

está he/she/it is; you are

estação *f* station; **estação alta** high season; **estação do ano** season; **estação dos autocarros** bus depot; bus station; **estação baixa** low season; **Estação de Caminho de Ferro (Esta. CF)** railway station; **estação do comboio** railway station; **estação final** terminus; **estação fluvial** river ferry port; **estação rodoviária** bus station; **estação de serviço** service station

Esta. CF *see* **estação**

estacionamento *m* parking; **estacionamento privado** private parking; **estacionamento proibido** no parking; **estacionamento reservado aos hóspedes** private car park – guests only

estacionar to park *(car)*

estadia *f* stay

estádio *m* stadium

Estados Unidos (EUA) *mpl* United States

estalagem *f* inn

estância *f*: **estância termal** spa

estar to be; **está bem** all right

estátua *f* statue

este (esta) this

estereofónico(a) stereo

esterilizar to sterilize

estes (estas) these

estômago *m* stomach; **o mal-estar de estômago** stomach upset

estores *mpl* blinds

estrada *f* road; **estrada encerrada ao tráfego** road closed; **estrada em mau estado** uneven road surface; **estrada florestal** forestry track; **estrada nacional (EN)** major road; national highway; **estrada principal** main road; **estrada com prioridade** priority; **estrada sem saída** no through road; **estrada secundária** minor road; **estrada de via dupla** dual carriageway

estragar to spoil

estrangeiro: no estrangeiro abroad

estrangeiro(a) *m/f* foreigner; **estrangeiros** non-nationals this way *(at airport, etc)*

estranho(a) strange

estreia *f* first showing

estreito(a) narrow

estuário m estuary

estudante m/f student

estufado(a) braised; stewed

estufa fria f glasshouse (in botanical gardens)

etiqueta f ticket; label

eu I

EUA see Estados Unidos

europeu (europeia) European

evitar to avoid

exceder to exceed; **não exceder a dose indicada** do not exceed the prescribed dose

excepto except; **excepto aos bombeiros** access for fire engines only; **excepto cargas e descargas das 8h às 13 horas** loading and unloading only 8 am till 1 pm; **excepto aos domingos** Sundays excepted; **excepto veículos públicos** public service vehicles only

excesso m : **excesso de bagagem** excess luggage

excursão f excursion; tour; **excursão guiada** guided tour

excursões fpl trips; excursions

exemplo m example; **por exemplo** for example

experimentar to try

expirar to expire

explicar to explain

explodir to explode

explosão f explosion

exportação f exportation

exportar to export

exposição f exhibition

exterior external

extintor m fire extinguisher

extremidade f edge

fábrica f factory

fabricado(a) em ... made in ...

faca f knife

face f cheek

fácil easy

facilidade f facility; **facilidades de pagamento** easy payments

facilitar to make easy

factura f invoice

fadista m/f 'fado' singer

fado m traditional Portuguese song

faiança f pottery

faisão m pheasant

faixa f lane (in road); **faixa da esquerda** outside lane; **faixa lateral** hard shoulder

falar to speak

falésias fpl cliffs

falhar: está a falhar the engine's misfiring

falta f lack; **falta de corrente** power cut

faltar to be lacking; **faltam dois** there are two missing

família f family

farinha f flour

farinheira f type of black pudding

farmácia f chemist's; **farmácia permanente** duty chemist; **farmácias de serviço** emergency chemists'

farófias fpl egg whites in milk dessert

faróis mpl headlights

farol m headlight; lighthouse

farolim m sidelight

farturas fpl long tube-like fritters

fatias douradas fpl egg and cinnamon bread pudding

fato m suit (man's); **fato de banho** swimsuit; bathing costume; **fato de ginástica** track suit; **fato de mergulhador** wetsuit; **fato de treino** track suit

favas fpl broad beans

favor m favour; **por favor** please; **é favor conferir o troco no acto de pagamento** please check that you have received the right change; **é favor fechar a porta** please close the door; **é favor não incomodar** please do not disturb

fazer to do; to make; **fazer a barba** to shave; **fazer a ligação** to get through (on phone); **fazem-se chaves** keys cut here; **faz favor** please

febras de porco fpl thin slices of pork

febre f fever; **febre dos fenos** hay fever

fechado(a) shut; closed; **fechado para balanço** closed for stocktaking; **fechado para férias** closed for holidays

fechar to shut; to close

feijão m beans

feijão-verde m French beans

feijoada f bean stew; **feijoada à alentejana** beans and mixed meat dish; **feijoada à algarvia** bean stew with pig's ear, black pudding and cabbage; **feijoada à transmontana** red beans and pork

feio(a) awful; ugly

feira f fair (commercial); market; **feira popular** fairground

feito(a): feito(a) à mão handmade; **feito(a) por medida** made-to-measure

fêmea f female (animals)

feminino(a) feminine

feriado m holiday; public holiday; **feriado nacional** bank holiday

férias fpl : **em férias** on holiday

ferida f wound

ferido(a) injured

ferragens fpl ironware

ferramenta f tool

ferro m iron; **ferro de engomar** iron (for clothes)

ferro-velho m scrap merchant

ferver to boil

festa f party (celebration); **festas dos santos populares** saints' feast days

Fevereiro m February

fiação f : **fiação e tecelagem** spinning and weaving

fiambre m ham

ficar to stay; to be; to remain

ficha f plug (electrical); **ficha dupla/tripla** adaptor (electrical)

fígado m liver; **fígado de porco à portuguesa** pig's liver in wine

figo m fig; **figos com amêndoas** figs with almonds; **figos secos** dried figs

fila f row (line)

filarmónica f brass band

filete m fillet steak; tenderloin; **filetes de pescada** hake steaks

filha f daughter

filho m son

filhozes fpl sugared buns; **filhozes**

de forma orange and port fritters

filial f branch *(of bank, etc)*

filigranas fpl filigree work

filme m film

filtro m filter; **com filtro** filter-tipped; tipped

fim m end; **ao fim de** at the end of; **fim de autoestrada** end of motorway; **fim de estação** end of season; **fim da proibição de estacionamento** end of parking restrictions; **fim de semana** weekend; **fim de traço de obras** end of roadworks

fio m wire; **fios de ovos** sugared filaments of egg yolk

fiscal m inspector

fita f tape; ribbon; **fita adesiva** adhesive tape; **fita gomada** sticky paper; **fita métrica** tape measure

fita-cola f Sellotape ®

fixar to fix

flanela f flannel

flash m flash

flipper m pinball machine

flor f flower

floresta f forest

florista f florist

focagem f : **focagem de faróis** headlight focus aligned

fogão m cooker

fogo m fire; **fogo!** fire!; **fogo de artifício** fireworks

folga f : **dia de folga** free day; day off

folha f leaf; **folha de alumínio** foil *(for cooking)*; **folha de estanho** tinfoil

folhados mpl puff pastries

folheto m leaflet

fome f : **tenho fome** I'm hungry

fonte f fountain; source

fora: **fora de** out of; **lá fora** outside; **para fora** out

força f power *(strength)*; force

forma f shape

formalidade f formality; **formalidades alfandegárias** customs formalities

formiga f ant

fornecer to supply

forno m oven; **no forno** in the oven

fortaleza f fortress

forte strong

fósforo m match

fotografia f photograph; print *(photograph)*

fotómetro m exposure meter

fraco(a) weak

frágil breakable

fralda f nappy; **fraldas descartáveis** disposable nappies; **fralda-calças** nappy pants

framboesa f raspberry

França f France

francês (francesa) French

frango m chicken; **frango à açoriana** chicken in onion sauce; **frango assado** roast chicken; **frango no churrasco** barbecued chicken; **frango no espeto** spit roast chicken; **frango frito/grelhado** fried/grilled chicken; **frango na púcara** chicken boiled in the pot; **frango no tacho** chicken casserole

frase f sentence

freguês (freguesa) m/f customer

frente *f* front; **em frente de** in front of; opposite; **sempre em frente** straight on

fresco(a) fresh; cool; crisp

frieira *f* chilblain

frigorífico *m* fridge; **com frigorífico e kitchenet** with fridge and cooking facilities

frio(a) cold

fritar to fry

frito(a) fried

fronha *f* pillow case

fronteira *f* border *(frontier)*

fruta *f* fruit

frutaria *f* fruit shop

fruto *m* fruit; **frutos secos e verdes** dried fruits and nuts

fuga *f* leak; **fuga de gás** gas leak

fumado(a) smoked

fumador(a) *m/f* smoker; **para não fumadores** non-smoking *(compartment, etc)*

fumar to smoke; **não fumar** no smoking; **não fume e desligue o motor** no smoking and switch off engine

fumo *m* smoke

funcionar to work *(machine)*; **não funciona** out of order

funcionário(a) *m/f* : **funcionário aduaneiro** customs officer

fundo *m* bottom

fundo(a) deep

furar to pierce

furnas *fpl* caverns

furto *m* theft

fusível *m* fuse

futebol *m* football

gabinete *m* : **gabinete de provas** changing room

gado *m* cattle; **gado bravo** beware – unfenced cattle

gaivota *f* seagull; pedal boat

galantine *f* : **galantine de coelho** cold rabbit roll; **galantine de galinha** cold chicken roll

galão *m* large white coffee

galeria *f* : **galeria de arte** art gallery

Gales *m* : **o País de Gales** Wales

galês (galesa) Welsh

galinha *f* hen; chicken; **galinha de fricassé** chicken fricassee

galo *m* cockerel

GALP *m* national petrol station

gamba *f* prawn

ganhar to earn; to win

ganso *m* goose

garagem *f* garage

garantia *f* guarantee; **garantia de cheques** cheque guarantee

gare *f* quay; platform

garfo *m* fork

garganta *f* throat

garoto *m* little boy; half black, half white coffee

garrafa *f* bottle

garrafão *m* five-litre bottle

gás *m* gas; **gás butano** butane gas; **gás campismo** camping gas; **a botija de gás** gas cylinder

gasóleo *m* diesel

gasolina *f* petrol; **gasolina normal** two-star petrol; **gasolina super** four-star petrol

gasosa *f* fizzy mineral water

gasoso(a) fizzy

gaspacho *m* chilled soup of tomato, cucumber and peppers

gastar to spend

gaveta *f* drawer

geada *f* frost

gelado *m* ice cream; ice lolly

gelar to freeze

gelataria *f* ice cream parlour

geleia *f* jelly

gelo *m* ice

gémeo(a) twin

género *m* kind; type

gengibre *m* ginger

gengivas *fpl* gums

gente *f* people; **toda a gente** everybody

geral[1] *f* gallery (in theatre)

geral[2] *adj* general

geralmente usually

gerência *f* management

gerente *m* manager

ginásio *m* gymnasium; gym hall

ginástica *f* gymnastics

ginginha *f* bitter cherry liqueur

ginja *f* cherry liqueur; **ginjas** bitter cherries

gin-tónico *m* gin and tonic

gira-discos *m* record player

girassol *m* sunflower

GNR *see* **guarda**

gola *f* collar

golfe *m* golf; **o campo de golfe** golf course; **o clube de golfe** golf club (place); **o taco de golfe** golf club (stick)

gordo(a) fat

gordura *f* fat

gorjeta *f* tip (to waiter, etc)

gostar: gostar de to like; **gosta?** do you like it?

gosto *m* taste

gotas *fpl* drops

Grã-Bretanha *f* Britain

grama *m* gramme

gramática *f* grammar

grande big; large; great

granizo *m* hail (weather)

grão *m* chickpeas

gratificação *f* tip

grátis free (costing nothing)

grau *m* degree (on scale)

gravador *m* tape recorder

gravata *f* tie

grave serious

grávida pregnant

gravidez *f* pregnancy

gravura *f* print (picture)

graxa *f* polish

grelha *f* grill

grelhado(a) grilled

grelhados *mpl* grilled dishes

grelos *mpl* sprouts

greve *f* strike (industrial); **em greve** on strike

gripe *f* flu

groselha *f* currant; redcurrant; blackcurrant; gooseberry

grosso(a) thick

grupo *m* group; party (group); **grupo sanguíneo** blood group

grutas *fpl* caves

guarda *m* : **guarda fiscal** coastguard; customs officer; **Guarda Nacional**

Republicana (GNR) National Guard
guarda-chuva m umbrella
guarda-lamas m mudguard
guardanapo m napkin
guarda-nocturno m night watchman
guardar to keep; to watch *(someone's luggage, etc)*
guarda-sol m sunshade
guia m/f guide; **guia intérprete** interpreter and guide; **guia turístico(a)** courier *(for tourists)*; tourist guide
guiar to drive
guiché m window *(at post office, bank)*
guisado m stew
guitarra f guitar

há there is; there are; **há vagas** vacancies
hamburguer m hamburger
hemorragia f haemorrhage
hemorróidas fpl haemorrhoids
higiene f hygiene
hipismo m horse racing; riding
história f history; story
hoje today; **hoje em dia** nowadays
homem m man
homens mpl Gents'
hóquei m hockey
hora f hour; time *(by the clock)*; **hora de chegada** time of arrival; **hora de partida** time of departure; **hora de ponta** rush hour; **que horas são?** what time is it?
horário m timetable; **horário de funcionamento** opening times;

horários dos ferry-boats ferry timetable
hortaliça f vegetables
hortelã f mint *(herb)*
hortelã-pimenta f peppermint *(herb)*
hóspede m/f guest
hospedeira f hostess; **hospedeira de bordo** stewardess; air hostess
húmido(a) damp

iate m yacht
icterícia f jaundice
idade f age; **que idade tem?** how old are you?
identificação f identification
idosos mpl the elderly; old people
ignição f ignition; starter *(in car)*; **a chave de ignição** ignition key
igreja f church
ilha f island
iluminado(a) floodlit *(building)*
imediatamente immediately
impedir to prevent
imperial m draught beer
impermeável m raincoat; waterproof
importação f importation
importância f importance; **não tem importância** it doesn't matter
importante important
importar: importa-se que ...? do you mind if ...?
imposto m tax; duty; **impostos** duty; tax; **imposto de selo não incluído** stamp duty not included; **imposto de valor acrescentado (IVA)** VAT
imprensa f the Press

impresso *m* form *(to fill in)*
imprevisto(a) unexpected
impulso *m* unit of charge *(for phone)*; **impulsos** dialled units
inauguração *f* opening
inaugurar to open
incêndio *m* fire
inchado(a) swollen
inchar to swell
incluído(a) included; **incluído jantar e uma bebida** a drink and a meal included in the price
inclusivamente inclusive
incomodar to disturb; **não incomodar** do not disturb
indemnizar to compensate
indicações *fpl* instructions for use
indicativo *m* dialling code; **indicativo europeu** dialling prefix for Europe; **indicativo inter-continental** dialling prefix for long-distance calls; **indicativo de país** dialling prefix for the country; **indicativo de zona** dialling prefix for the town
indigestão *f* indigestion
indivíduo *m* person
infantário *m* kindergarten
infecção *f* infection
infeccioso(a) infectious *(illness)*
infelizmente unfortunately
inflamação *f* inflammation
inflamável *f* inflammable
informação *f* information; **informação turística** tourist information
informações *fpl* information office; **informações/secção de**

informações enquiry desk/office; **para informações e reclamações marcar …** for information or complaints dial …
informado(a) well-informed
informar to inform
infracção *f* offence
Inglaterra *f* England
inglês (inglesa) English
íngreme steep
iniciais *fpl* initials
iniciar to begin
início *m* beginning; **início de autoestrada** start of motorway
inquilino *m* tenant
inscrever to register
insecticida *f* fly-killer
insecto *m* insect
insolação *f* heatstroke; sunstroke
instalações *fpl* facilities; **instalações de tradução simultânea** simultaneous translating facilities
instituto *m* institute
insuflável inflatable
inteiro(a) whole
interdito(a) forbidden; **interdito m/18 anos** under 18s strictly not admitted; **interdito a menores de … anos** no admission to those under … years of age
interessado(a) interested
interessante interesting
interessar to interest
interesse *m* interest
interior inside
intermediário *m* middleman
interno(a) internal

intérprete *m/f* interpreter
interruptor *m* switch
intervalo *m* interval *(in theatre)*
intestinos *mpl* bowels
intoxicação *f* food poisoning
introduzir to introduce; **introduza a moeda no ranhura** insert coin in slot
inundação *f* flood
inválido(a) invalid
inverno *m* winter
inversão de marcha *f* U-turn
iogurte *m* yoghurt
ir to go
Irlanda *f* Ireland; **a Irlanda do Norte** Northern Ireland
irlandês (irlandesa) Irish
irmã *f* sister
irmão *m* brother
iscas *fpl* : **iscas fritas com batatas** fried liver and French fries; **iscas de porco** marinated pig's liver; **iscas à portuguesa** beef liver
isolar to isolate
isqueiro *m* lighter
isso that
isto this
Itália *f* Italy
italiana *f* espresso coffee
italiano(a) Italian
itinerário *m* route
IVA *m* VAT

já already
Janeiro *m* January
janela *f* window
jantar *m* dinner; evening meal; **jantares e ceias** evening meals and dinners served
jardim *m* garden; **jardim botânico** botanical garden; **jardim infantil/de infância** kindergarten; **jardim zoológico** zoo
jardineira *f* vegetable stew
jazz *m* jazz
joalharia *f* jeweller's; jewellery
joelho *m* knee
jogar to play
jogo *m* game; gambling; play; **jogo de dardos** darts
jóia *f* jewel; **jóias** jewellery
jornal *m* newspaper
jovem young
Julho *m* July
Junho *m* June
juntar to join
junto near; **junto ao aeroporto** close to the airport
juventude *f* youth

kg. *see* **quilo(grama)**
kispo *m* nylon anorak; child's jumpsuit

lá there; **lá em baixo** downstairs
lã *f* wool; **lã de vidro** fibreglass
lábio *m* lip
laca *f* lacquer
laço *m* bow *(ribbon, string)*
lacticínios *mpl* dairy products
ladeira *f* slope
lado *m* side; **ao lado de** beside
ladrão *m* thief
Lafões area renowned for its fruity

red and white wines

lagarto m lizard

lago m lake

lagosta f lobster; **lagosta à americana** lobster with tomato and onions

lagostim m crayfish

lamento I'm sorry

lâminas de barbear fpl razor blades

lâmpada f light bulb

lampreia f lamprey eel; **lampreia à moda do Minho** whole lamprey in a thick sauce; **lampreia de ovos** dessert made of eggs and sugar

lançar to throw

lanchar to go for something to eat

lanche m luncheon; light afternoon meal

lápis m pencil; **lápis de cera** crayons

lar m home

laranja f orange; **o doce de laranja** marmalade; **cor de laranja** orange (colour)

lareira f fireside

largo m small square

largo(a) broad; loose (clothes); wide

largura f width

lasanha f lasagne

lata f tin; can (of food)

latão m brass

lavabo m lavatory; toilet; **lavabos** toilets

lavagante m a kind of lobster

lavagem f: **lavagem e mise** shampoo and set; **a lavagem automática** car wash

lava-louça m sink

lavandaria f laundry; **lavandaria automática** launderette; **lavandaria a seco** dry-cleaner's; **lavandaria e tinturaria** laundry and dyer's

lavar to wash (clothes, etc); **lavar a louça** to wash up; **lavar à mão** to handwash; **lavar as mãos** to wash one's hands

lavável washable

laxativo m laxative

lebre f hare

legumes mpl vegetables

lei f law

leilão m auction

leitão m sucking pig; **leitão assado** roast sucking pig; **leitão da Bairrada** sucking pig from Bairrada

leitaria f dairy

leite m milk; **com leite** white (coffee); **leite achocolatado** chocolate-flavoured milk drink; **leite condensado** condensed milk; **leite creme** egg custard; **leite desnatado** skimmed milk; **leite evaporado** evaporated milk; **leite gordo** full cream milk; **leite de limpeza** cleansing milk; **leite magro/meio gordo** skimmed/semi-skimmed milk; **leite pasteurizado** pasteurized milk; **leite em pó** powdered milk; **leite ultrapasteurizado** UHT milk

lembranças fpl souvenirs

leme m rudder

lenço m handkerchief; tissue; **lenço de papel** paper tissue

lençol m sheet

lente f lens; **lentes de contacto** contact lenses

lentilhas fpl lentils

lento(a) slow

leque *m* fan

ler to read

leste *m* east

letra *f* letter

letreiro *m* sign

levantar to draw *(money)*; to lift; **levante o auscultador** lift the receiver

levar to take

leve light *(not heavy)*

libra *f* pound; **libras esterlinas** pounds sterling

lição *f* lesson

licença *f* permit; **com licença** excuse me

liceu *m* secondary school

licor *m* liqueur; **licores** wines and spirits; **licor de medronho** strawberry liqueur; **licor de ovo** advocaat; **licor de peras** pear liqueur; **licor de whisky** Drambuie ®

ligação *f* connection *(trains, etc)*; **ligação com ...** connects with ...; **ligações intercontinentais** international connections; **ligações para outros destinos** connections for other destinations

ligado(a) on *(engine, gas, etc)*

ligadura *f* bandage; **ligadura adesiva** Elastoplast ®

ligeiro(a) light; **ligeiros** light vehicles

lima[1] *f* lime *(fruit)*

lima[2] *f* file; **lima das unhas** nailfile

limão *m* lemon

limite *m* limit; **limite de peso autorizado** luggage allowance;

limite de velocidade speed limit

limonada *f* lemonade

limpar to wipe; to clean

limpa-vidros *m* window-cleaning liquid

limpeza *f* cleaning; **limpeza a seco** dry-cleaning

limpo(a) clean

língua *f* language; tongue; **língua de porco** tongue of pork; **língua de fricassé** tongue; **língua de vaca** tongue of beef

linguado *m* sole *(fish)*; **linguado no forno** baked sole; **linguado frito** fried sole; **linguado grelhado** grilled sole; **linguado à meunière** sole meunière

linguiça *f* spicy pork sausage

linha *f* line; thread; platform *(railway)*; **linha aérea** airline; **linha jovem** young people's fashions

linho *m* linen

liquidação *f* (clearance) sale

líquido *m* liquid; **líquido para a louça** washing-up liquid

Lisboa (Lx) Lisbon

liso(a) smooth

lista *f* list; **lista de preços** price list; **lista telefónica** telephone directory

litoral *m* seaboard

litro *m* litre

livraria *f* bookshop

livre free; vacant

livrete *m* car documents

livro *m* book; **livro de cheques** cheque book

lixa *f* sandpaper

lixívia *f* bleach

lixo m rubbish

local m site; **local de interesse turístico** place of interest to tourists; **local sossegado** quietly situated

localidade f place; town

loção f lotion

loja f shop; **loja de ferragens** ironmonger's; **loja franca** duty-free shop

lombo m : **lombo de porco** pork loin; **lombo de vaca** sirloin

Londres London

longa metragem f full length feature film

longe far; **longe de** far from; **é longe?** is it far?; **mais longe** farther

longo: ao longo da rua along the street

lotação f : **lotação esgotada** sold out (tickets)

lotaria f lottery; **lotaria nacional** state lottery

louça f dishes; crockery

louro(a) fair (hair)

lua f moon

lua-de-mel m honeymoon

lubrificantes mpl lubricants

lucro m profit

lugar m seat (in theatre); space (room); place; **lugares marcados em todas as sessões** all seats numbered in every session; **lugares em pé** standing room; **lugares reservados a acompanhantes de crianças com menos de 4 anos** seats reserved for those with children under four; **lugares reservados a cegos e inválidos** seats reserved for blind

people and the disabled; **lugares reservados a grávidas** seats reserved for expectant mothers

lulas fpl squid; **lulas de caldeirada** squid in onion, potato, nutmeg and wine sauce; **lulas com natas** stewed squid in cream; **lulas recheadas** squid stuffed with bacon and onion; **lulas à sevilhana** fried squid in batter

luvas fpl gloves

luxo m luxury; **de luxo** de luxe

luxuoso(a) sumptuous

luz f light; **luzes de presença** sidelights; **luzes de perigo** hazard lights

Lx see **Lisboa**

M. underground (railway)

má see **mau**

maçã f apple; **maçã assada** baked apple

maçapão m marzipan

maçaroca f corn on the cob

macarrão m macaroni

macedónia de frutas f fruit cocktail

macho m male (animal)

macio(a) soft

maço m : **maço de cigarros** packet of cigarettes

madeira f wood

Madeira f island renowned for its fortified wines

madrugada f early morning

maduro(a) ripe

mãe f mother

magoar: magoar alguém to hurt

someone; **magoar-se** to hurt oneself

magro(a) thin

Maio m May

maionaise f mayonnaise

maior larger; **a maior parte de** the majority of; **para maiores de 16 anos** for over-16's only

maiôts mpl knitwear

mais more; **o/a mais** the most

mal wrong; evil

mala f suitcase; bag; trunk

malagueta f chilli

mal-entendido m misunderstanding

mal-estar m discomfort

malhas fpl knitwear

malmequer m marigold

mancha f stain

mandar to send

maneira f way (method)

manga f sleeve

manhã f morning

manicura f: **manicura e pedicura** manicurist and chiropodist

manteiga f butter; **manteiga meio sal** slightly salted butter

mantar to keep

manter-se: mantenha-se à direita, caminhe pela esquerda keep to the right, walk on the left

mão f hand

mapa m map; **mapa das estradas** road map; **mapa das ruas** street plan

maquilhagem f make-up

máquina f machine; **máquina de**

filmar movie camera; cine camera; **máquina fotográfica** camera

mar m sea

maracujá m tropical fruit

marca f brand; **marca registada** registered trade mark

marcação f booking; dialling

marcar to dial (phone number); to book (hotel, etc); **marcar o número** to dial the number

marcha-atrás f reverse (gear)

Março m March

marco do correio m pillar box

maré f tide

maré-baixa f low tide

maré-cheia f high tide

marfim m ivory

margarina f margarine

margem f bank; edge

marido m husband

marinada f marinade

marinha f navy

marisco m seafood; shellfish

marisqueira f shellfish restaurant

marmelada f quince preserve

marmelo m quince; **marmelos assados** baked quince

mármore m marble (substance)

marque: marque o número desejado dial the number you want

Marrocos Morocco

marroquinaria f leather goods

mas but

masculino m male

massa f dough; **massas** pasta; **massa folhada** puff pastry

mata f forest

maternidade *f* maternity hospital

matraquilhos *mpl* table football

matrícula *f* number plate

mau (má) bad

máximo(a) maximum

mazagran *m* iced coffee and lemon

me me

mecânica *f* **geral** general repairs

mecânico *m* mechanic

média *f* average

medicamento *m* medicine

médico(a) *m/f* doctor

medida *f* measure; size

médio(a) medium

medir to measure

medusa *f* jellyfish

meia *f* sock

meia-hora *f* half-hour

meia-idade: de meia-idade middle-aged

meia-noite *f* midnight

meias *fpl* stockings; **meias de vidro** hosiery

meio *m* middle; **no meio de** in the middle of

meio(a) half; **meio bilhete** half fare; **meia desfeita** cod and chickpeas; **meia garrafa** a half bottle; **meia de leita** glass of milk; **meia pensão** half board; **duas e meia** half past two

meio-dia *m* midday; noon

meio-seco medium sweet *(wine)*

mel *m* honey

melancia *f* watermelon

melão *m* melon; **melão com presunto** melon and ham

melhor best; better

meloa *f* small melon; **meloa com vinho do Porto/da Madeira** small melon with Port/Madeira wine

menina *f* Miss; girl

menino *m* boy

menor smaller

menos least; less

mensagem *f* message

menstruação *f* period *(menstruation)*

mercado *m* market; **mercado municipal** town market

mercearia *f* grocer's

merengue *m* meringue

mergulho *m* dive

mês *m* month

mesa *f* table

mesmo(a) same; even

mesquita *f* mosque

metade *f* half; **metade do preço** half price

meter to put; to place

metro *m* metre; underground *(railway)*

metropolitano *m* underground *(railway)*; tube *(underground)*

meu (minha) my

mexer to move; **não mexer** do not touch

mexilhão *m* mussel

micróbio *m* germ

migas *fpl* **: migas à alentejana** thick bread soup

mil thousand; **mil folhas** sweet flaky pastry

milhão *m* million

milho m maize

minha see **meu**

mini-mercado m small supermarket

mínimo(a) minimum

minúsculo(a) tiny

miolos mpl (sheep's) brains; **miolos com ovos** brains with eggs

mistura f mixture; petrol/oil mix (two-stroke)

misturar to mix

miúdos mpl : **miúdos de cabrito** offals of kid in garlic sauce

mobília f furniture

mochila f backpack; rucksack

moda f fashion; **modas** fashion wear

moeda f coin; currency

moído(a) ground (coffee, etc)

moinho m windmill; **moinho de café** coffee grinder

mola f peg; spring (coiled metal)

moleja f soup made with pig's blood

molhado(a) wet

molhar to soak

molho m sauce; gravy; **molho bearnaise** sauce made from egg yolk, lemon juice and herbs; **molho bechamel** béchamel sauce; **molho branco** white sauce; **molho de cogumelos** creamed mushroom sauce; **molho cor-de-rosa** creamy tomato sauce; **molho à espanhola** spicy onion and garlic sauce; **molho holandês** hollandaise sauce; **molho ao Madeira** Madeira wine sauce; **molho mornay** béchamel sauce with cheese; **molho**

mousseline hollandaise sauce with cream; **molho tártaro** tartar sauce; **molho de tomate** tomato and onion purée; **molho velouté** white sauce with egg yolks and cream; **molho vinagrete** vinaigrette

momento m moment; **(só) um momento** just a moment

montanha f mountain

montante m amount (total)

montra f shop window

morada f address

moradia f villa

morango m strawberry; **morangos com chantilly** strawberries and whipped cream

morar to live; to stay

morcela f black pudding

mordedura f : **mordedura de insecto** insect bite

morder to bite

mortadela f spicy sausage

mosaicos mpl mosaic tiles

mosca f fly (insect)

moscatel m muscatel wine

mostarda f mustard

mosteiro m monastery

mostrador m dial; glass counter

mostrar to show

mota f motorbike

motocicleta f motorbike

motor m engine; motor; **motor de arranque** starter motor; **motor fora de borda** outboard motor

motorista m driver

motorizada f motorbike

Mouraria f Moorish quarter

Mouros mpl Moors (people)

mousse f mousse; styling mousse; **mousse de fiambre** ham soufflé

móveis mpl furniture

muçulmano(a) Muslim

muito very; much; quite (rather); very much; **muito obrigado** thank you very much

muitos(as) a lot (of); many; plenty (of)

mulher f female; woman; wife

multa f fine

multidão f crowd

mundial world

mundo m world

muralhas fpl ramparts

muro m wall

museu m museum; **museu de arte** art gallery

música f music

nabo m turnip

nacional national

nacionalidade f nationality

nada nothing; **nada a declarar** nothing to declare

nadador salvador m lifeguard

nadar to swim

namorada f girlfriend

namorado m boyfriend

não no; not; **não é?** isn't it?

não-alcoólico(a) nonalcoholic

napolitanas fpl long biscuits

nariz m nose

nata f cream; custard

natação f swimming

Natal m Christmas

naturalidade f place of birth

natureza f nature

navio m ship

neblina f mist

necessidade f need

negar to refuse

negativo(a) negative

negócios mpl business

negro(a) black

nem: nem ... nem ... neither ... nor ...

nenhum(a) none

nêspera f loquat

neta f granddaughter

neto m grandson

neve f snow; **coberto de neve** snowed-up

névoa f mist

nevoeiro m fog

ninguém nobody

nível m level

nó m knot; **nó rodoviário** motorway interchange

No. see **número**

nocivo(a) harmful

nódoa f stain; **nódoa negra** bruise

noite f evening; night; **à noite** in the evening; **a noite de Santo António** festival on 13 June; **a noite de São João** festival on 24 June; **a noite de São Pedro** festival on 29 June; **noites de gala** gala evenings

nome m name; **nome próprio** first name

nordeste m north east

normalmente usually

noroeste m north west

norte m north

nos us

nós we

nosso(a) our

nota f note; banknote

notar to notice

notícia f piece of news

Nova Zelândia f New Zealand

nove nine

Novembro m November

novo(a) new; young

noz f nut; walnut

noz-moscada f nutmeg

nu(a) naked

nublado(a) dull *(weather)*; cloudy

número (No.) m number; size *(of clothes, shoes)*; **número de telefone** phone number

nunca never

nuvens fpl clouds

o the; him

objecto m object; **objectos perdidos** lost property; lost and found

obra-prima f masterpiece

obras fpl roadworks

obrigado thank you

obrigatório(a) compulsory

obter to get

oceano m ocean

ocidental western

oculista m optician

óculos mpl glasses; **óculos de sol** sunglasses

ocupado(a) busy; engaged *(telephone, toilet)*; occupied

oeste m west

oferecer to offer

oferta f offer; **oferta especial** special offer

ofício m occupation

oito eight

olá hello

olaria f pottery

óleo m oil; **óleo dos travões** brake fluid

oleoso(a) greasy

olhar: olhar (para) to look (a); **olhe** look

olho m eye

omeleta f omelette; **omeleta de camarão** shrimp omelette; **omeleta de cogumelos** mushroom omelette; **omeleta com ervas** vegetable omelette; **omeleta de fiambre** ham omelette; **omeleta de presunto** gammon omelette; **omeleta de queijo** cheese omelette

onda f wave *(on sea)*

onde where

ontem yesterday

optar to choose

óptimo(a) excellent

ora now; well now

orçamento m budget; **orçamentos grátis** free estimates

ordenado m wage

orelha f ear; **orelha de porco assada** roast pig's ear; **orelha de porco de vinagrete** pig's ear in vinaigrette

organizado(a) organized

orquídea f orchid

os the; them

osso m bone

ostra f oyster; **ostras ao natural** oysters; **ostras recheadas** oysters stuffed with a sauce made with egg yolks

otorrinolaringólogo *m* ear, nose and throat specialist

ou or

ourivesaria *f* : **ourivesaria e joalharia** goldsmith's and jeweller's

ouro *m* gold; **de ouro** gold *(made of gold)*

outono *m* autumn

outro(a) other; **outra vez** again

Outubro *m* October

ouvido *m* ear

ouvir to hear; to listen (to)

ovelha *f* sheep

ovo *m* egg; **ovo bem cozido** hard-boiled egg; **ovo cozido** boiled egg; **ovo escalfado** poached egg; **ovo escalfado sobre tostas** poached egg on toast; **ovo em geleia** jellied egg; **ovo pouco cozido** soft-boiled egg; **ovo quente** soft-boiled egg; **ovos estrelados** fried eggs; **ovos mexidos** scrambled eggs; **ovos mexidos à portuguesa** scrambled eggs with peppers, tomato and garlic; **ovos moles** egg dessert; **ovos verdes** fried stuffed eggs

oxigénio *m* oxygen

paço *m* palace; **paço ducal** duke's palace

pacote *m* packet

padaria *f* baker's

pagamento *m* payment; **pagamento a prestações** hire purchase; **pagamento a pronto** cash payment

pagar to pay

página *f* page; **páginas amarelas** Yellow Pages

pago(a) paid

pai *m* father; parent

paio *m* type of salami

país *m* country

pais *mpl* parents

paisagem *f* scenery

palácio *m* palace

palavra *f* word

pálido(a) pale

palito *m* toothpick

panadinhos de pescada *mpl* fish cakes

panado(a) fried in breadcrumbs

panela *f* pan; pot

pano *m* cloth

panqueca *f* pancake

pão *m* bread; loaf; **pão de centeio** rye bread; **pão integral** wholemeal bread; **pão de ló** sponge cake; **pão de milho** maize bread; **pão torrado** croutons; **pão de trigo** wheat bread

papel *m* paper; **papel de carta** writing paper; **papel de embrulho** wrapping paper; brown paper; **papel higiénico** toilet paper

papelaria *f* stationer's

papos de anjo *mpl* eggs baked in kirsch

papo-seco *m* roll *(of bread)*

par *m* pair

para for; towards; to

parabéns *mpl* congratulations; happy birthday

pára-brisas *f* windscreen

pára-choques *m* bumper

parafuso *m* screw

paragem f stop (for bus, etc);
paragem proibida no waiting;
paragem zona fare stage

parar to stop

pare: pare, escute e olhe stop, look
and listen; **pare ao sinal vermelho**
stop when lights are red

parede f wall

parente m relation (family)

pargo m sea bream; **pargo assado**
roast bream; **pargo cozido** boiled
bream

parque m park; **parque de
campismo** campsite; **parque de
campismo para caravanas** caravan
site; **parque de estacionamento** car
park; **parque de estacionamento
subterrâneo** underground car park;
parque florestal forestry park;
parque infantil play group; **parque
de merendas** picnic park; **parque
privativo** private parking; **parque
recreativo** amusement park

parquímetro m parking meter

parrilhada f grilled fish

particular private

partida f departure; start; **partidas**
departures

partir to break; to leave; **a partir
de ...** from ...

Páscoa f Easter

passa f raisin

passadeira f zebra crossing; **na
passadeira dê prioridade aos peões**
give way to pedestrians on the
crossing

passado m the past

passado(a): mal passado underdone
(steak); **bem passado** well done

(steak)

passageiro m passenger;
passageiros passengers this way

passagem f: **passagem de nível**
level-crossing; **passagem de peões**
pedestrian crossing; **passagem
proibida** no right of way; **passagem
subterrânea** underpass

passaporte m passport; **o controle
de passaportes** passport control

passar to pass

pássaro m bird

passatempos mpl entertainment;
hobbies

passe[1] m season ticket; **passe social**
travel pass

passe[2] go (when crossing road); walk

passear to go for a walk

passeio m walk; pavement; **passeio
de barco** boat trip; **passeio a cavalo**
pony trekking

pasta f paste; **pasta dentífrica**
toothpaste

pastéis mpl cakes; croquettes;
pastéis de bacalhau cod croquettes;
pastéis de tentugal custard tart with
almonds

pastel m pie; pastry (cake); **pastel
folhado** puff pastry cake

pastelaria f pastry; café; cake shop;
pastelaria e confeitaria baker's and
confectioner's

pastilha f pastille; **pastilha elástica**
chewing gum; **pastilhas para a
garganta** throat lozenges; **pastilha
de mentol** mint (sweet)

pataniscas fpl salted cod fritters

paté m pâté; **paté de aves** chicken
pâté; **paté de fígado** liver pâté; **paté**

de galinha chicken pâté; **paté de lebre** hare pâté

patinagem f skating (ice); roller-skating

patinar to skate

pátio m courtyard

pato m duck; **pato com arroz** duck and rice with Port and white wine sauce; **pato assado** roast duck; **pato com laranja** duck in orange sauce

pau m stick

pavimento m : **pavimento escorregadio** slippery (road) surface

pé m foot; **a pé** on foot; **ao pé de** near

peão m pedestrian

peça[1] f part; play; **peças e acessórios** spares and accessories

peça[2]: **peça folhetos** ask for a leaflet; **peça informações** ask for information

pechincha f bargain (good buy)

pediatra m/f paediatrician

pedir to ask; **pedir alguma coisa** to ask for something; **pedir a alguém para fazer** to ask someone to do; **pedir emprestado** to borrow

peito m breast; chest

peixaria f fish shop

peixe m fish; **peixe congelado** frozen fish

peixe-espada m swordfish; **peixe-espada de escabeche** marinated swordfish; **peixe-espada de fricassé** swordfish fricassee

pele f fur; skin

película f film (for camera)

pena[1] f feather

pena[2] f pity

penalidade f penalty

pendurar to hang up (clothes)

penhasco m cliff

penicilina f penicillin

pensão m boarding house; guesthouse; **pensão completa** full board; **pensão residencial** boarding house

pensar to think

penso m sticking plaster; **penso higiénico** sanitary towel

pente m comb

penteado m hairstyle

peões mpl pedestrians

pepino m cucumber; **pepino de conserva** gherkin

pequeno(a) little; small; **pequeno almoço** breakfast

pera f pear; **pera abacate** avocado pear

perceber to understand; **percebe?** do you understand?

percebes mpl edible barnacles

percurso m route

perdão I beg your pardon; I'm sorry

perder to lose; to miss (train, etc)

perdido(a) lost; **perdidos e achados** lost and found; lost property

perdiz f partridge; **perdizes assadas no forno** roast partridges; **perdizes de escabeche** marinated partridges; **perdizes estufadas** partridges rolled in ham and cooked with onion and carrot; **perdizes fritas** fried partridges; **perdizes na púcara** casseroled partridges

perfumaria f perfume shop

perguntar to ask

perigo *m* danger; **perigo de incêndio** fire hazard; **perigo de morte** extreme danger

perigoso(a) dangerous

permanecer to stay

permanente *f* perm

permissão *f* permission

permitir to allow

perna *f* leg; **perna de carneiro assada** roast leg of lamb; **perna de carneiro entremeada** stuffed leg of lamb; **pernas de rã** frogs' legs

pérola *f* pearl

perto: perto de near

peru *m* turkey; **peru assado** roast turkey; **peru de fricassé** turkey fricassee; **peru recheado** stuffed turkey

pesado(a) heavy; **pesados** heavy vehicles

pesar to weigh

pesca *f* fishing; **pesca desportiva** competition fishing; **pesca à linha** line fishing; **pesca submarina** spear fishing

pescada *f* hake; **pescada cozida** boiled hake

pescadinhas *fpl* whiting; **pescadinhas de rabo na boca** whiting with their tail in their mouth

pescar to fish

peso *m* weight; **peso líquido** net weight

pêssego *m* peach

pessoa *f* person; **pessoas** people

pessoal[1] *m* staff

pessoal[2] *adj* personal

petiscos *mpl* snacks

petróleo *m* oil

peugas *fpl* socks

pezinhos de coentrada *mpl* pig's trotters in coriander sauce

picada *f* sting

picado(a) stung

picante spicy

pilha *f* pile; battery *(for torch)*

pílula *f* the pill

pimenta *f* pepper

pimento *m* pepper *(vegetable)*

pingue-pongue *m* table tennis

pinha dourada *f* meringue dessert

pinhal *m* pine wood

pintado: pintado à mão hand-painted; **pintado de fresco** wet paint

pintar to paint

pintura *f* painting

pionés *m* drawing pin

pipi *m* cooked sparrow

piripiri *m* hot chilli dressing

pisca-pisca *m* indicator *(on car)*

piscina *f* swimming pool; **piscina aberta** outdoor swimming pool; **piscina aquecida** heated swimming pool; **piscina coberta** indoor swimming pool; **piscina para crianças** paddling pool; **piscina de mar aquecida** heated sea-water swimming pool

piso *m* road surface; **piso escorregadio** slippery road surface; **piso irregular** uneven road surface

pista *f* track; runway

pistão *m* piston

planear to plan

planta f plant

planta (de Lisboa) f street map (of Lisbon)

plástico m plastic

plataforma f platform

plateia f stalls (in theatre)

platinados fpl points (in car)

pneu m tyre; **a pressão dos pneus** tyre pressure

pó m dust; powder; **pó de talco** talcum powder

poço m well

poder to be able; can

pois yes, of course

polegar m thumb

polícia[1] f police; **Polícia de Segurança Pública (PSP)** the Portuguese police

polícia[2] m policeman; police officer

polidesportivo m sports centre

poluição f pollution

poluído(a) polluted

polvo m octopus

pomada f ointment; **pomada para o calçado** shoe polish

pomar m orchard

pombo m pigeon

ponte f bridge

ponteagudo(a) pointed

popa f stern (of boat)

população f population

por by (through); **por aqui/por ali** this/that way; **por hora** per hour; **por pessoa** per person

pôr to put

porção f portion

porcelana f porcelain; china

porco m pig; pork

por favor please

pormenores mpl details

porquê why

porta f door; **porta telecomandada** automatic door; **a porta No. ...** gate number ...

porta-bagagens m boot (of car); luggage rack

porta-chaves m key ring

portagem f toll; **portagem a 6 kilómetros** 6 km to pay toll

porta-moedas m purse

portátil portable

porteiro m porter

porto[1] m harbour; **porto de pesca** fishing port

porto[2] m port (drink)

Porto m : **o Porto** Oporto; **o vinho do Porto** Port wine

português (portuguesa) Portuguese

positivo(a) positive

posologia f dose

possível possible

postal f postcard

posta-restante f poste restante

posto m post; job; **posto clínico** first aid post; **posto de socorros** first aid centre

pouco(a) little

poupar to save (money, time)

pousada f state-run hotel

povo m people

povoação f village

praça f square (in town); **praça de**

táxis taxi rank; **praça de touros** bullring

praia f beach; seaside

prancha f sailboard; **prancha de saltos** diving board; **prancha de surf** surfboard

prata f silver

prato m dish; plate; course *(of meal)*; **prato da casa** speciality of the house; **prato do dia** today's special

prazer m pleasure; **prazer em conhecê-lo** pleased to meet you

preçário m price list

precipício m cliff

precisar to need; **é preciso** it is necessary

preço m price; **preço por dia** price per day; **preço por mês** price per month; **preço por pessoa** price per person; **preço por semana** price per week; **preço de venda por atacado** wholesale price; **preço de venda a retalho** retail price; **preços especiais fora de época** special off-season prices; **preços especiais para longas estadias** special prices for long stays; **preços de ocasião** bargain prices; **preços reduzidos** reduced prices

prédio m building

preencher to fill in

preferência: de preferência rather

preferir to prefer

prego m beef cutlet; **pregos (no pão)** beef rolls

prejuízo m damage

pré-mamã m maternity wear

prémio m prize

prenda f gift

preocupado(a) worried

pré-pagamento pay before you eat

preparado(a) ready

preparar to prepare

presente m gift; present

pressão f pressure; **pressão dos pneus** tyre pressure

prestar: preste atenção pay attention; **não presta** it is no good

presunto m ham

preto(a) black

prima f cousin *(female)*

primavera f spring *(season)*

primeiro(a) first; **primeiro andar** first floor; **primeira classe** first class *(seat etc)*; **primeiros socorros** first aid

primo m cousin *(male)*

principal main

principiante m/f beginner

princípio m beginning

prioridade f priority; **prioridade à direita** give way to the right

prisão f prison; **com prisão de ventre** constipated

privado(a) private

proa f bow *(of ship)*

procissão f procession

procurar to look for

produto m product; proceeds; **produtos alimentares** foodstuffs; **produtos expostos são para consumo da casa** items on display are for consumption on the premises only; **produtos de limpeza** cleaning products; **produtos naturais** health foods

professor(a) m/f teacher

profissão f profession; **profissão, idade, nome** profession, age and name

profundidade f depth

profundo(a): pouco profundo shallow

proibido(a) forbidden; **proibido acampar** no camping; **proibido afixar cartazes** stick no bills; **proibida a entrada** keep out; no entry; **proibida a entrada a menores de … anos** no admittance to those under … years of age; **proibida a entrada a pessoas estranhas ao serviço** staff only; **proibido estacionar** no parking; **proibido fumar** no smoking; **proibido a paragem** no stopping; **proibida a passagem** no access; **proibido pisar a relva** do not walk on the grass; **proibido tirar fotografias** no photographs; **proibido tomar banho** no bathing

projecção f: **projecção de filmes** film show; **projecção de gravilha** loose chippings

promoção f special offer

pronto(a) ready

pronto-a-comer takeaway

pronto-a-vestir ready-to-wear

pronto-socorro m breakdown van

propina f fee

proporção f rate

propósito m intention

propriedade f estate (property)

proprietário m owner

protecção f protection

protector da pele m skin protection cream

proteger to shelter; **proteger do calor e da humidade** store in a cool dry place

prótese dentária m dental fittings

prova f proof; **prova (de vinho)** sampling (of wine)

provar to taste; to try on

provável likely

província f province

provisório(a) temporary

próximo(a) near; next; **próxima sessão às … horas** next performance at …

prudente careful (prudent)

PSP see **polícia**

público m audience

público(a) public

pudim m pudding; **pudim de amêndoa** almond pudding; **pudim flan** crème caramel; **pudim molotov** caramel and whipped egg white; **pudim de peixe** fish baked in a mould

pulmão m lung

pulover m sweater; pullover

pulsação f pulse

pulseira f bracelet; wrist strap

pulso m wrist

pura lã f pure wool

puré m : **puré de batata** mashed potato; **puré de castanhas** chestnut purée

purificador do ar m air freshener

puxar to pull; **puxar a alavanca em caso de emergência** pull lever in case of emergency; **puxar o autoclismo** to flush (toilet)

puxe pull

quadro *m* picture; painting

qual which; **qual é?** which is it?

qualidade *f* quality

qualquer: qualquer medicamento deve estar fora do alcance dascrianças keep all medicines out of reach of children

quando when

quantia *f* amount

quantidade *f* quantity

quanto how much; **quantos(as)?** how many?; **quanto tempo?** how long? *(time)*

quarta-feira *f* Wednesday

quarto[1] *m* room; bedroom; **quartos alcatifados** carpets in all rooms; **quarto de banho** bathroom; **quarto com duas camas** twin-bedded room; **quarto de casal** double room; **quarto para duas pessoas** double room

quarto[2] fourth; quarter; **um quarto de hora** a quarter of an hour

quatro four

que what; **o que é?** what is it?

quebra-mar *m* pier

quebrar to break; **quebrar em caso de emergência** break in case of emergency

queda *f* fall; **queda de pedras** falling rocks

queijada *f* cheesecake; **queijadas de Tomar** almond cup cakes

queijo *m* cheese; **queijo de Azeitão** soft, smooth cheese; **queijo de cabra** goat's milk cheese; **queijo de Castelo Branco** sheep's milk cheese; **queijos e doces** cheeses and desserts; **queijo fresco** mild goat's milk cheese; **queijo da Ilha** peppery cheese from the Azores; **queijo de ovelha** sheep's milk cheese; **queijo do Pico** cow's milk cheese; **queijo Rabaçal** sheep's milk cheese; **queijo saloio** sheep's milk cheese; **queijo de São Jorge** cow's milk cheese; **queijo de Serpa** cheese with a strong smell and taste; **queijo da Serra** sheep's milk cheese; **queijo da Serra da Gardunha** goat's milk cheese

queimadura *f* burn; **queimadura do sol** sunburn *(painful)*

queixa *f* complaint

quem who; **de quem é?** whose is it?

quente hot; warm

querer to want; to wish

quilo(grama) (kg.) *m* kilo

quilómetro *m* kilometre

quinquilharias *fpl* **: quinquilharias e velharias** bric-à-brac and curios

quinta *f* farm

quinta-feira *f* Thursday

quiosque *m* kiosk; newsstand

quotidiano(a) daily

R. *see* **rua**

rã *f* frog

rabanadas *fpl* French toast

rabanete *m* radish

Radiodifusão *f* **: Radiodifusão Portuguesa (RDP)** Portuguese Radio

radiografia *f* X-ray

Radiotelevisão *f* **: Radiotelevisão Portuguesa (RTP)** Portuguese Television

râguebi *m* rugby

raia *f* skate *(fish)*

raiva *f* rabies

raíz f root
rali m rally(-driving)
rampa f ramp
rapariga f girl
rapaz m boy
rápido m express *(train)*
rápido(a) fast
raposa f fox
raqueta f racket
rasgar to tear
ratazana f rat
rato m mouse
R/C *see* **rés-do-chão**
RDP *see* **Radiodifusão**
rebentar to blow *(fuse, light bulb)*; to burst
reboques mpl towing service; breakdown service
rebuçado m sweet *(confectionery)*
recado m message
recauchutado m retread
receber to receive
receita f receipe; **receita médica** prescription
receitar to prescribe
recepção f desk *(in hotel, etc)*; reception
recheio m filling *(in cake, etc)*; stuffing
recibo m receipt
recinto m : **em recinto coberto** indoors *(sports, etc)*
reclamação f reclaim; complaint; **reclamações** complaints; **reclamação de bagagem** baggage reclaim
recolha f delivery

recolher to collect
recomendar to recommend
recomendável advisable
recompensa f reward
reconhecer to recognize
recordação f souvenir
recordar-se to remember
recostável reclining
rede f net; **rede de autocarros** bus network
redução f reduction; discount
reduza a velocidade reduce speed; slow
reembolsar to reimburse
refeição f meal; **refeição da casa** set menu; **refeições ligeiras** light meals; snacks
refogado fried in oil with garlic and vinegar
reformado(a) m/f senior citizen; pensioner
refrescos mpl refreshments
regatas fpl boat races
região f area *(region)*; **região demarcada** official wine-producing region *(on wine label)*
registar to register
regressar to come back
regulamentos mpl regulations
Reino Unido m United Kingdom
relógio m watch; clock
relojoaria f watchmaker's shop
relva f grass; **não pisar a relva** keep off the grass
remédio m medicine; remedy
remetente m sender
renda[1] f lace; **rendas de bilros**

handwoven lacework

renda² f rent

reparação f repair; **reparações** repairs

reparar to fix; to repair

repelente m insect repellent

repolho m cabbage

representação f performance

requeijão m curd cheese

rés-do-chão (R/C) m ground floor

reserva f reservation; booking; **reserva de hotéis e apartamentos** hotel and apartment reservations; **reserva de lugar** seat reservation; **reserva natural** nature reserve; **reservas e passagens** tickets and reservations

reservado(a) reserved

reservar to book (room, sleeper); to reserve

residência f boarding house; residence

residir to live

respirar to breathe

responder to answer; to reply

responsável responsible

resposta f answer

restaurante m restaurant; **restaurante panorâmico** restaurant with a view

retalho m oddment; **vender a retalho** to retail

retirar: retirar o auscultador do descanso lift the phone off the hook

retrosaria f haberdashery

revelação f development (of photos)

revelar to develop (photos)

reverso m the other side

revisor m ticket collector

revista f magazine

ria f river mouth

ribeiro m stream

rímel ® m mascara

rins mpl kidneys; **rins ao Madeira** kidneys in Madeira wine sauce

rio m river

riscas: às riscas striped

risco m risk

rissol m rissole; **rissóis de camarão** shrimp rissoles

RN see **rodoviária**

robalo m rock bass

rochas fpl rocks

roda f wheel

rodovalho m turbot

rodoviária f: **Rodoviária Nacional (RN)** national bus company

rojões mpl cubes of pork; **rojões à minhota** fried pork loins in red pepper sauce

rolha f cork

rolo m cartridge (for camera); roll; **rolos** roll of film; **rolo de carne** meat loaf; **rolo a cores** colour film

rosé m light, dry or sweet wine

rosto m face

roteiro m guidebook; **roteiro de bolso** pocket guide

roubar to steal; to rob

roupa f clothes; **roupas** clothes; **roupa interior** underwear

roxo(a) purple

RTP see **radiotelevisão**

rua (R.) f street
rubéola f German measles
ruído m noise
ruínas fpl ruins; **ruínas romanas** Roman remains
rumo m direction
ruptura f break

S. see **São**
sábado m Saturday
sabão m soap; **sabão em flocos** soapflakes; **sabão em pó** soap powder
saber to know (fact)
sabonete m soap (perfumed)
sabor m flavour; taste
sacarina f saccharin
saca-rolhas m corkscrew
saco m bag; handbag; **saco cama** sleeping bag; **saco do lixo** bin bag; **saco de viagem** flight bag; travel bag
safio m sea eel
saia f skirt
saída f exit; **saídas** departures; **saída de emergência** emergency exit; **saída de veículos – não estacionar** exit – keep clear
sair to go out; to come out
sal m salt
sala f room; **sala de banho** bathroom; **sala de bingo** bingo hall; **sala de chá** tea room; **sala de conferências e banquetes** conference and banquet hall; **sala de convívio** lounge; **sala de divertimentos** amusement arcade; **sala de embarque** lounge (at airport); **sala de espera** waiting

room; **sala de espera para partidas** departure lounge; **sala de estar** living room; lounge (in hotel, house); **sala de jantar** dining room; **sala de jogos** playroom; amusement hall; **sala de reunião** meeting hall; **sala de televisão** TV lounge; **com sala de conferências e de projecção** with conference hall and projection facilities
salada f salad; **salada de agrião** watercress salad; **salada de alface** lettuce salad; **salada de atum** tuna and potato in egg sauce; **salada de chicória** chicory salad; **salada de frutas** fruit salad; **salada mista** mixed salad; **salada de ovas** fish roe salad; **salada de pepino** cucumber salad; **salada de pimentos** green pepper salad; **salada à portuguesa** tomato, peppers, carrot, onion, beetroot, egg, cucumber and radish salad; **salada russa** Russian salad; **salada de tomate** tomato salad
salão m hall (for concerts, etc); **salão de beleza** beauty salon; **salão de chá** tea room; **salão de convívio** lounge; **salão de festas** function suite
saldo m sale (of bargains); **saldos** sales
salgado(a) salty
salmão m salmon; **salmão fumado** smoked salmon
salmonete m mullet; **salmonetes grelhados** grilled mullet
salpicão m salami sausage; spicy sausage
salsa f parsley
salsicha f sausage; **salsicha de**

Frankfurt frankfurter; **salsichas de peru** turkey sausages; **salsichas de porco** pork sausages

salsicharia f delicatessen

salteado(a) sautéed

salvar to rescue; to save *(rescue)*

salva-vidas m lifeboat

salvo(a) safe

sandálias fpl sandals

sandes f sandwich; **sandes de fiambre** ham sandwich; **sandes de lombo** steak sandwich; **sandes mista** mixed sandwich; **sandes de paio** sausage sandwich; **sandes de presunto** ham sandwich; **sandes de queijo** cheese sandwich

sanduíche f sandwich

sangrar to bleed

sangue m blood

sanitários mpl toilets

Santa (Sta.) f saint

Santo (Sto.) m saint

santo(a) holy

santola f spider crab

São (S.) m Saint

sapataria f shoe shop

sapateira f a kind of crab

sapateiro m shoemaker

sapato m shoe; **sapatos e malas** leather goods *(shoes and cases)*

saquinhos de chá mpl tea bags

sarampo m measles

sardinha f sardine; **sardinhas assadas** grilled sardines; **sardinhas assadas na brasa** charcoal-grilled sardines

satisfeito(a) happy; satisfied

saudação f greeting

saudades fpl : **ter saudades** to be homesick

saudar to greet

saudável healthy

saúde f health; **saúde!** cheers!

se¹ if; **se bebeu não conduza** don't drink and drive; **se faz favor (SFF)** please

se² himself; herself; yourself; themselves

sé f cathedral

secador m dryer; **secador de cabelo** hair dryer

secar to dry; to drain *(tank)*; **não secar à máquina** do not spin dry

secção f department *(in store)*; **secção de criança** children's department; **secção de perdidos e achados** lost-property office

seco(a) dry

secretaria f general office

secretária f secretary

século m century

seda f silk

sede f thirst; **ter sede** to be thirsty

segmento m piston ring

seguinte following

seguir to follow; **seguir pela direita** keep to your right; **seguir pela esquerda** keep to your left

segunda-feira f Monday

segundo m second *(time)*

segundo(a) second; **segundo andar** second floor; **de segunda classe** second class *(seat, etc)*; **em segunda mão** second-hand

segurança f safety

segurar to hold

seguro *m* insurance; **seguros** insurance services; **seguro de fronteira** green cards here; **seguro contra terceiros** third party insurance; **seguro contra todos os riscos** comprehensive insurance; **seguro de viagem** travel insurance

seguro(a) safe *(medicine, beach)*; reliable *(method)*; sure

seio *m* breast

seis six

selecção *f* selection

seleccionar to choose

selo *m* stamp; **selo de garantia** seal of guarantee

selvagem wild

sem without; **sem corantes nem conservantes** does not contain artificial colouring or preservatives; **sem entrada e sem juros em 12, 18 ou 24 meses** no deposit and interest free for 12, 18 or 24 months

semáforos *mpl* traffic lights

semana *f* week; **para a semana/na semana passada** next/last week; **por semana** weekly *(rate, etc)*

semanal weekly

semelhante similar

sempre always

senha de saída *f* ticket *(at the cinema, disco)*

senhor *m* sir; **Senhor** Mr

senhora *f* lady; madam; **Senhora** Mrs, Ms; **senhoras** Ladies'

senhoria *f* landlady *(of property)*

senhorio *m* landlord *(of property)*

sensação *f* feeling; sensation

sensacional terrific

sentar-se to sit (down)

sentido *m* sense; meaning; **sentido único** one-way street

sentir to feel

separar to separate

ser to be

serra *f* mountain range

serviço *m* service; room service; service charge; cover charge; **serviço de quartos** room service; **com serviço à carta e ementa do dia** we serve both à la carte and menu of the day; **serviço expresso** express service; **serviço (não) incluído** service (not) included; **serviços de informação** information service; **serviço de peças** spare parts service; **serviço permanente** 24-hour service; **serviço de pneus** tyre service; **serviço de pronto-socorro** breakdown service; **serviço rápido** speedy service; **serviço de roboque** breakdown service; **serviço de recepção e relações com o público** reception and public relations service; **serviço telegráfico** telegraph service

servir to serve; **serve-se das ... horas às ... horas** meals served from ... o'clock until ... o'clock

sessão *f* session; performance

sesta *f* siesta

sete seven

Setembro *m* September

seu (sua) his; her; your

sexo *m* sex

sexta-feira *f* Friday

SFF *see* se¹

shampô *m* shampoo

si you

sidra *f* cider

significar to mean

silêncio *m* silence

sim yes

simpático(a) nice

sinagoga *f* synagogue

sinal *m* signal; deposit *(part payment)*; **sinal de alarme** communication cord; **sinal de impedido** engaged tone; **sinal de marcação** dialling tone; **sinal de tocar** ringing tone; **sinal de trânsito** road sign

sinalização *f* system of traffic signs

sino *m* bell

sintoma *m* symptom

sirva-se: sirva-se à temperatura ambiente serve at room temperature; **sirva-se fresco** serve cool; **sirva-se gelado** serve chilled

sistema *m* system; **sistema de arrefecimento** cooling system

sítio *m* place; spot

situação *f* situation

situado(a) situated

smoking *m* dinner jacket

só only; **só pode vender-se mediante receita médica** available only on prescription

sobre over; **sobre o mar** overlooking the sea

sobrecarga *f* excess load; surcharge

sobremesa *f* dessert

sobressalente: a peça sobressalente spare part; **a roda sobressalente** spare wheel

sobretudo *m* overcoat

sócio *m* member; partner

socorro *m* : socorro! help!; **socorro 115** emergency service 999; **socorros e sinistrados** accidents and emergencies

soirée *f* evening performance *(cinema, etc)*

sol *m* sun

solha *f* flounder; **solha assada no forno** baked flounder; **solha frita** fried flounder; **solha recheada** stuffed flounder

solteiro(a) single *(not married)*

solúvel soluble

som *m* sound

soma *f* amount *(sum)*

sombra *f* shadow *(in sun)*

sonhos *mpl* milk and egg fritter

sono *m* sleep

sopa *f* soup; **sopa de agriões** cress soup; **sopa alentejana** egg, bread, garlic and coriander soup; **sopa de alho francês** leek soup; **sopa de amêijoas/conquilhas** clam/baby clam soup; **sopa de camarão** thick shrimp soup; **sopa de carne** bone soup with carrots, peas and turnip; **sopa de cebola gratinada** onion soup au gratin; **sopa de cozido** meat soup; **sopa do dia** soup of the day; **sopa dourada** egg-based dessert; **sopa de espargos** asparagus soup; **sopa de espinafres** spinach and potato soup; **sopa de feijão-verde** green bean soup; **sopa de grão** chickpea soup; **sopa Juliana** vegetable soup; **sopa de lagosta**

lobster soup; **sopa de legumes** fresh vegetable soup; **sopa de ostras** oyster soup; **sopa de ovo** boiled eggs in potato and onion purée; **sopa de pão e coentros** soup with bread and coriander; **sopa de pedra** tomato soup with spicy sausage, beans and poatoes; **sopa de peixe** fish soup; **sopa de pescada** fish head soup; **sopa de rabo de boi** oxtail soup; **sopa de sangue de porco** pig's blood and liver soup; **sopa de tartaruga** turtle soup; **sopa de tomate** cream of tomato soup; **sopa de tomate alentejana** tomato soup with bread, eggs, onion and garlic

soporífero *m* sleeping pill

soprar to blow

sorte *f* luck; fortune; **boa sorte** good luck

sorvete *m* water-ice

sótão *m* attic

soufflé *m* soufflé; **soufflé de camarão** prawn soufflé; **soufflé de cogumelos** mushroom soufflé; **soufflé de peixe** fish soufflé; **soufflé de queijo** cheese soufflé

soutien *m* bra

sozinho(a) alone

Sta. *see* **Santa**

steak *m* steak

Sto. *see* **Santo**

sua *see* **seu**

suave mild

subida *f* rise; ascent

subir to go up

subterrâneo(a) underground

subúrbio *m* suburb

sudeste *m* south east

sudoeste *m* south west

suficiente enough

sujar to dirty; to stain

sul *m* south

sumo *m* juice; **sumo de frutas** fruit juice; **sumo de laranja** orange juice; **sumo de maçã** apple juice; **sumo de toranja** grapefruit juice

suor *m* sweat

superfície *f* area; surface

supermercado *m* supermarket

suplemento *m* supplement; **suplemento quarto individual** extra charge for single room

suplente *m* substitute

supositório *m* suppository

surdo(a) deaf

surf *m* surfing

tabacaria *f* tobacconist's; newsagent

tabaco *m* tobacco

tabela *f* list; table

taberna *f* wine bar

tabuleiro *m* tray

tabuleta *f* sign

taça *f* cup

tacão *m* heel

tal such

talão *m* voucher

talco *m* talc

talheres *mpl* cutlery

talho *m* butcher's

talvez perhaps

tamanho *m* size

também also; too

tamboril *m* frogfish

tampa *f* lid; cover; top; cap

tampões *mpl* tampons

tangerina *f* tangerine

tanto(a) so much

tão so

tapeçaria *f* carpet weaving

tapete *m* carpet; rug; **tapete rolante** baggage reclaim; **tapetes e carpetes** rugs and carpets; **tapetes de Arraiolos** traditional rugs

tarde¹ *f* afternoon

tarde² late *(in the day)*

tarifa *f* charge; **tarifas na portagem** toll charges

tarte *f* tart; **tarte de amêndoa** almond tart; **tarte de maçã** apple tart

tasca *f* tavern; wine bar

taxa *f* fee; **taxa de juro** interest rate; **taxa normal** peak-time rate; **taxa reduzida** off-peak rate; **taxa das comunicações telefónicas** dialling rates

tax-free duty-free

táxi *m* taxi

te you

teatro *m* theatre

tecelagem *f* weaving

tecido *m* fabric; tissue; cloth

técnico *m* technician

tejadilho *m* roof rack

telecomandado(a) remote-controlled

teleférico *m* cable car

telefone *m* telephone

telefonema *m* phone call

telefonista *f* operator

telegrafar to telegraph

telegrama *m* telegram

telejornal *m* newscast; bulletin

televisão *f* television

televisor *m* television set

telhado *m* roof

temperatura *f* temperature

tempero *m* dressing *(for salad)*; spice

tempestade *f* storm

tempo *m* weather; time *(duration)*

temporada *f* season

temporário(a) temporary

tencionar to intend

tenda *f* tent

ténis *m* tennis; **ténis de mesa** table tennis

tenro(a) tender *(meat)*

tensão *f* tension; **tensão arterial alta/baixa** high/low blood pressure

tentar to try

tentativa *f* attempt; effort

tépido(a) tepid; lukewarm

ter to have; **ter febre** to have a temperature

terça-feira *f* Tuesday

terceiro(a) third; **terceiro andar** third floor; **para a terceira idade** for the elderly

terço *m* third

termas *fpl* spa

termo *m* (vacuum) flask

termómetro *m* thermometer

terra *f* earth; land; ground

terraço *m* veranda; balcony

terramoto *m* earthquake

terreno *m* ground; land

tesoura *f* scissors

tesouro *m* treasure
testemunha *f* witness
tetina *f* teat
têxteis *mpl* textiles
ti you
tigelada *f* cream cake
tímido(a) shy
tingir to dye
tinta *f* ink; paint
tinturaria *f* dry-cleaner and dyer's
típico(a) typical
tipo *m* sort; kind
tira-nódoas *m* stain remover
tirar to remove; to take out *(tooth)*
tiro *m* shot; **tiro aos pratos e pombos** clay pigeon shooting
toalha *f* towel; **toalha de mesa** tablecloth
toalhete *m* : **toalhetes refrescantes** baby wipes; **toalhete de rosto** face cloth; flannel *(for washing)*
tocar to touch; to play
todo(a) all; **toda a gente** everyone; **todas as coisas** everything; **em toda a parte** everywhere
tomada *f* socket; power point; **tomada para a máquina de barbear** shaving point
tomar to take; **tomar banho** to bathe; to take a bath; **tomar banhos de sol** to sunbathe; **tomar antes de se deitar** to be taken before going to bed; **tomar em jejum** take on an empty stomach; **tomar a seguir às refeições** to be taken after meals; **tomar ... vezes ai dia** to be taken ... times a day
tomate *m* tomato; **tomate pelado** peeled tomatoes; **tomatoes recheados** stuffed tomatoes
tomilho *m* thyme
tonelada *f* ton
tontura *f* dizziness
toque please ring
toranja *f* grapefruit
torcer to twist; to turn
tornar: tornar-se sócio de to join *(club, etc)*
torneio *m* tournament
torneira *f* tap
tornozelo *m* ankle
torrada *f* toast
torrão de açúcar *m* lump of sugar
torre *f* tower
torresmos *mpl* small rashers of bacon
torta *f* tart *(cake)*; **torta de camarão** shrimps in egg fritter roll; **torta de laranja** orange roll
tortilha *f* Spanish omelette
torto(a) twisted
tosse *f* cough
tosta *f* : **tosta mista** toasted ham and cheese sandwich; **tosta de queijo** toasted cheese sandwich; **tostas** French toast
tostões *mpl* : **25 tostões** = 2.5 escudos
totobola *m* football pools
totoloto *m* lottery
toucinho *m* bacon; **toucinho do céu** almond and egg roll
tourada *f* bullfight
touro *m* bull
tours de autocarro *mpl* coach tours

tóxico(a) poisonous *(substance)*; toxic

trabalhar to work *(person)*

trabalho *m* work; **trabalhos na estrada** roadworks

tradicional traditional

tradução *f* translation

tradutor(a) *m/f* translator

traduzir to translate

tráfego *m* traffic

traje *m* : **traje regional** regional dress

trajecto *m* journey; course

tranquilo(a) calm; quiet

transferência *f* transfer

transferir to transfer

transgressão *f* traffic offence

trânsito *m* traffic; **trânsito condicionado** restricted traffic; **trânsito congestionado** heavy traffic; **trânsito fechado** road blocked; **trânsito proibido** no entry; **trânsito nos dois sentidos** two-way traffic

transpiração *f* perspiration; sweat

transporte *m* transport

transtorno *m* upset; inconvenience

trás: para trás backwards; **no banco de trás** in the back *(of car)*; **a parte de trás** back

tratamento *m* treatment

travar to brake

travessa *f* lane *(in town)*

travesseiro *m* pillowcase

travessia *f* crossing *(voyage)*

travões *mpl* brakes

trazer to bring

treinador *m* coach *(instructor)*

trela *f* lead *(dog's)*

tremer to shiver

três three

trespassa-se business for sale

triângulo *m* warning triangle

tribunal *m* court

tricotar to knit

trigo *m* wheat

tripas *fpl* tripe; **tripas à moda do Porto** tripe Oporto style

tripulação *f* crew

triste sad

troca *f* exchange; swap

trocar to exchange; to change

troco *m* change *(money)*

tropa *f* army

trovoada *f* thunderstorm

trufas *fpl* truffles

truta *f* trout; **truta assada no forno** baked trout

tu you

tubo *m* exhaust pipe; tube; hose *(in car)*

tudo everything

túnel *m* tunnel

turismo *m* tourism; tourist information office; **turismos ligeiros** light vehicles this way

turista *m/f* tourist

ultimamente lately; recently

último(a) last

ultrapassagem *f* overtaking; **proibida a ultrapassagem** no overtaking

ultrapassar to overtake; to pass

um(a) a; an; one
unha f nail (on finger, toe)
união f junction
unicamente only; **unicamente para adultos** for adults only
único(a) single (not double)
unidade f unit (hi-fi, etc)
unir to join
universidade f university; college
urbano(a) urban
urgência f urgency; **urgências** emergencies; emergency hospital
urgente: é urgente it is urgent
urgentemente urgently
urtiga f nettle
usado(a) used (car, etc)
usar to use; **use sempre o cinto** always wear a seat belt
uso m use; **uso externo** for external use
utentes mpl : **utentes com bilhete** ticket holders this way
útil useful
utilização f use
utilizar to use
uva f grape

vaca f cow
vacina f vaccination
vagão m railway carriage; coach
vagão-restaurante m buffet car
vagar to be vacant; **a casa vaga em Dezembro** the house will be vacant in December
vago(a) vague
vale¹ m valley
vale² m : **vale postal** postal order

valer to be worth
validação f : **validação de bilhetes** punch your ticket here
válido(a) valid; **válido até** valid until
valioso(a) valuable
valor m value
válvula f valve
vapor m steam
varanda f veranda; balcony; **varandas com vista para o mar e a montanha** balconies overlooking the sea and mountains
variado(a) varied
varicela f chickenpox
vários(as) several
vaso m vase; **vasos e faianças tradicionais** traditional pottery
vazio(a) empty
veado m deer; **veado assado** roast venison
vedar to stop up (hole, leak, etc); **vedado ao trânsito** no thoroughfare
vegetação f Vegetation
vegetal m vegetable; **vegetais congelados** frozen vegetables
vegetariano(a) vegetarian
veículo m vehicle; **veículos longos** long vehicles; **veículos pesados** heavy goods vehicles
vela¹ f sail; sailing
vela² f spark plug; candle
velho(a) old
velocidade f gear; speed; **velocidade limitada** speed limit in force; **velocidade máxima … km/h** maximum speed … km/h
velocímetro m speedometer

vencimento *m* wage

venda *f* sale *(in general)*; **venda de cadernetas** prepaid tickets sold here; **venda por grosso e a retalho** wholesalers and retailers; **venda de passagens aéreas** plane ticket sales; **venda proibida** not for public sale; **vendas e reparações** sales and repairs; **venda através do correio** mail order; **venda através do telefone** telephone selling

vendedeira *f* seller

vendedor *m* seller; **vendedor de jornais** newsagent

vender to sell; **vende-se** for sale

veneno *m* poison

venenoso(a) poisonous *(snake)*

ventilação *f* ventilation

vento *m* wind; **vento fraco ou moderado** winds light to moderate

ventoinha *f* fan *(electric)*

ver to see; to watch *(TV)*

verão *m* summer

verdade *f* truth; **não é verdade?** isn't it?

verdadeiro(a) true

verde green

vergas *fpl* wicker goods

verificar to check

vermelho(a) red

vermute *m* vermouth

verniz *m* varnish; **verniz das unhas** nail polish

verso *m* back *(of cheque, of page)*

vertigem *f* dizziness

vespa *f* wasp

véspera *f* the day before; the eve

vestiário *m* cloakroom; changing room

vestíbulo *m* entrance hall

vestido *m* dress; **vestido de saia e casaco** suit *(woman's)*

vestígio *m* sign

vestir to dress; to wear

vestuário *m* clothes; **vestuário impermeável** waterproof clothing

veterinário(a) *m/f* vet

vez *f* time; **às vezes** occasionally; sometimes; **uma vez** once; **duas vezes** twice; **cada vez mais** more and more; **muitas vezes** often

via¹ *f* lane; **via rápida** dual carriageway

via²: **via aérea** by air mail; **via nasal** to be inhaled; **via oral** orally

viaduto *m* viaduct

viagem *f* trip; journey; **viagem de autocarro** coach trip; **viagem de barco** boat trip; **viagem organizada** package tour

viajante *m/f* traveller

viajar to travel

viatura *f* vehicle

vida *f* life

vidros *mpl* glassware; **vidros e escapes** windscreens and exhausts; **vidros pára-brisas** replacement windscreens

vila *f* town; **vila de pescadores** fishing village

vinagre *m* vinegar

vindima *f* harvest *(of grapes)*

vinho *m* wine; **vinho de aperitivo** aperitif; **vinho branco** white wine; **vinho de casa** house wine; **vinho clarete** light red wine; **vinho comum** ordinary wine; **vinho doce**

sweet wine; **vinho espumante** sparkling wine; **vinho espumoso** sparkling wine; **vinho de Madeira** Madeira wine; **vinho de mesa** table wine; **vinho moscatel** muscatel wine; **vinho do Porto** port wine; **vinho da região** local wine; **vinho rosé** rosé wine; **vinho seco** dry wine; **vinho tinto** red wine; **vinho verde** semi-sparkling acid wine; **vinho de Xerez** sherry

vinte twenty; **vinte e quatro horas serviço de quartos** 24-hour room service

viola f guitar

violino m violin

vir to come

virar to turn; **vire à direita** turn right; **vire à esquerda** turn left

visita f visit; **visita a lugares de interesse** sightseeing

visitante m/f visitor

visitar to visit

vista f view

visto m visa

vistoso(a) gorgeous; attractive

vitela f veal; **vitela assada** stewed veal; **vitela com cogumelos** veal in mushroom sauce; **vitela estufada** roast veal

viúva f widow

viúvo m widower

vivenda f chalet; villa (by the sea)

viver to live

vivo(a) alive

vizinho(a) m/f neighbour

você you

vocês you (plural)

volante m steering wheel

voleibol m volleyball

volta f turn; **à volta de** about; **em volta de** around

voltagem f voltage

voltar to return (go back); to come back; **volto já** I will be back in a minute

vomitar to vomit

vontade f will; **à vontade** at ease

voo m flight; **voo fretado** charter flight; **voo normal** scheduled flight

vos you; to you

vós you

voz f voice

vulcão m volcano

WC m : **WC privativo** private toilet

wind-surf m windsurfing

xadrez m chess

xarope m syrup; **xarope de morango** strawberry liqueur; **xarope para a tosse** cough medicine

xerez m sherry

zona f zone; **zona azul** permitted parking zone; **zona de banhos** swimming area; **zona interdita** no thoroughfare

NOTES